The Sustainable Entrepreneur

The Unconventional Model for Personal Financial Freedom

The Sustainable Entrepreneur

The Unconventional Model for Personal Financial Freedom

Brian M. Allen

First Edition: Mar 2024

ISBN 9798879873894

This is book is dedicated to my wife, Aleta.

Thank you for being my

best friend,

business partner,

editor,

and my eternal love.

You make the journey worth the effort!

Contents

INTRODUCTION 9

**SECTION 1: MAKE IT, MANAGE IT, AND THRIFT IT: 3
STEPPING-STONES TO FREEDOM** 12

CHAPTER 1: ENTREPRENEURSHIP - MICROBUSINESS 13
Benefits of Business Ownership 18
The Real Reasons to Own Your Own Home-Based Business.....22
Developing a Personal Mission Statement 23
I Want to Start My Own Business, What Should I Do?.............25
CHAPTER 2: MONEY MANAGEMENT 29
Financial Literacy is a Lifelong Quest 43
CHAPTER 3: THRIFT 46

**SECTION 2: FEED ME AND JUST IN CASE: FOOD
FREEDOM & PREPARATION** 64

CHAPTER 4: GARDENING 66
CHAPTER 5: FOOD RESERVES AND PRESERVATION 74
CHAPTER 6: EMERGENCY PREPAREDNESS 81
Avoiding Data Emergencies 81
Physical & Mental Emergency Preparation 84

**SECTION 3: GIVING AND GETTING: THE CORE OF
HEART FREEDOM** 88

CHAPTER 7: VOLUNTEERING FOR A BALANCED LIFE.....................89
CHAPTER 8: SKILLS DEVELOPMENT (THE LINCHPIN STEPPING
STONE) 95

**SECTION 4: BUILDING A FOUNDATION AND ACTION
PLAN** 103

CHAPTER 9: PILLAR TO SUCCESS: RECOGNIZE A HIGHER POWER
....104
CHAPTER 10: THE FIRST STEP 109
EPILOGUE..111

Introduction

If you have dreamed of owning your own business, you should know you are not the only one. The Small Business Administration (SBA) notes there are over 33.1 million small businesses in the United States. In 2023, small businesses accounted for the creation of 62.7% of new jobs in the United States. An amazing 78% of all those were small businesses with fewer than 10 employees. And surprisingly enough Experian, the credit reporting agency, found the average age of small business owners is not 20, 25, 30, or 35 but 50.3 years old. In other words, wanting to start a business in your late 40s, 50s, or later is perfectly acceptable. However, you are going to have to accept that venturing out on your own is not without the potential for some naysayers. You, however, need not join the naysayers.

While some people may sometimes vilify entrepreneurs and say that it is simply another word for being unemployed, the facts reveal a far different picture. Entrepreneurs get and keep our economy rolling. From before the founding of the United States as a nation, entrepreneurship has been what defines Americans as American. The 1607 Virginia Company founding of Jamestown, Virginia, was a joint-stock company with shared risks and the pooling of resources for the opportunity of gain for all involved. Even today, the United States has the third highest entrepreneurship rate in the world lagging only two countries (the United Arab Emirates and Saudi Arabia). Yet even in third place for entrepreneurship, the United States represents the largest single national economy in the world with a whopping 25.4 billion dollar gross domestic product (GDP) in 2022. If 62.7% of new jobs in the United States are created by small business, it is critical to the success of the country economically. Simply put, the U.S. economy cannot grow without small business creation and ownership. It is the engine of growth personally, locally, and nationally. Government programs and large businesses simply do not have the flexibility or agility needed to create dramatic community, state, and national economic growth. National economic strength is built on the freedoms afforded individuals to create and maintain their own wealth. That wealth is the fountain from which we feed our families, communities, nation, and the world. For those who wish to manage their own destiny, starting, running, and growing their own company may be the realization of a dream. Yet, that dream is the embodiment of the oldest and longest enduring of American Dreams. A dream the founders of the United States shared and preserved for us today. Starting your own business and defending the right to define your own future is the greatest gift you can give to your family and the rest of the world.

As you begin your journey toward small business ownership, keep in mind you will be part of a select group of individuals. These are the real builders and providers in our economy. Perhaps you are looking at this from a far simpler standpoint. Business ownership for you is a personal journey. It comes from the desire to improve your life and your personal economic means. You dream of the ability to have more money than you have month instead of more month than you have money. You dream of the ability to tell your boss that he or she is fired. Regardless of your motivation, this book is for you. This book is designed to help you start on your journey and then sustain your efforts, no matter what happens along the way. The point of your journey as a sustainable entrepreneur is not to build a future and lose it. The grand goal is to start, maintain, and grow into your desired future through your small business.

This book was born from a personal journey of freedom to create my own vision of my future and to make a difference for existing and future business owners. That desired freedom is financial as well as physical. Like you, I came to realize that my entrepreneurial desires and dreams of something better would never come from working for someone else alone. Even if it meant I had to start part time to get to my final destination. I understood that I had to practice the principles of free enterprise and define what freedom meant to and for me.

My own journey is far from over, and I find as I take each step there are new and exciting opportunities. I wrote this book to share what I have learned from my previous entrepreneurial attempts, some successful and some failures, and to achieve my desired liberty from debt. My journey took from starting out in the U.S. Air Force to being a full-time online college professor. I now teach professionally what it took me lots of years to learn, and a lot of money paid to earn the get degrees to teach others and convince myself and others I knew what I was talking about. What I will share here should save you from making many of the same mistakes I made along the way, and you will not need to spend 10 years going to college for a doctorate to learn and apply these lessons. In the end, I hope you will find that you are not alone in your desire for earned freedom. My hope is that what I share will inspire you to plan for more than just another way to make more money. The plans, map, and journey you take will be your own and are part of your destiny, but your impact may just change your future, your family's future, your community, and our nation. If you are going to dream big; go all the way!

Section 1: Make it, Manage it, and Thrift It: 3 Stepping-Stones to Freedom

This book is broken into four sections for organization and simplicity. Section 1 deals with how to make more money through starting a small business, principles for managing your money, and applying thriftiness to save more money. Section 2 focuses on how you can prepare for potential slowdowns, feeding yourself while you readjust your business, and being prepared for practical life emergencies. In Section 3, we will discuss ways to improve your life and the lives of your fellow beings through volunteering and personal skills development. Finally, in Section 4, we will talk about recognizing and surrendering to a higher power as a pillar to our lives, businesses, communities, and nation. These ideas are encapsulated in the following diagram which is called the Freedom Matrix.

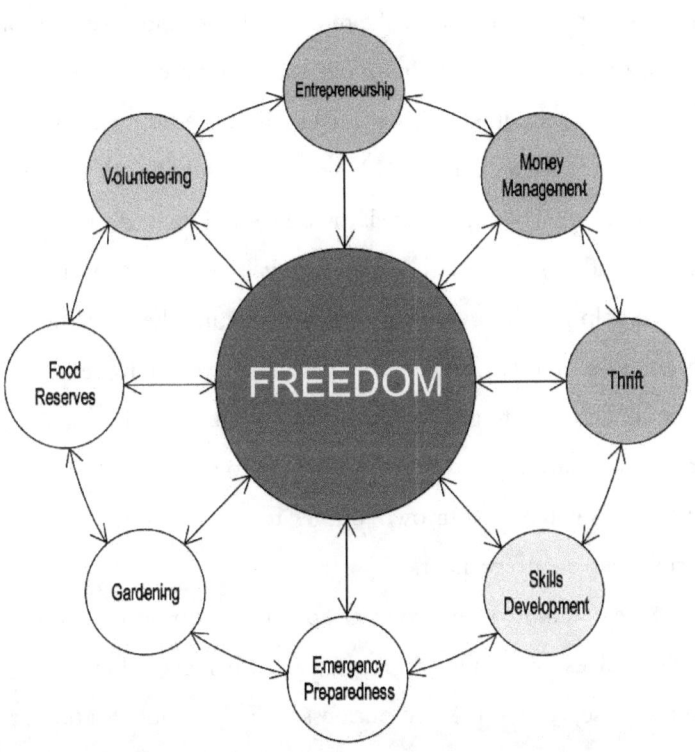

Chapter 1: Entrepreneurship - Microbusiness

Businesses are supposed to make money. That sounds like a simple and straightforward concept, right? While this might seem like a rudimentary statement, it is the root of why businesses are started and run. No one ever said, well no one I have ever consulted with ever said, I want a business where I am busy all the time and I make no money. No one ever said this because the idea is crazy. The purpose of this chapter is to help you discover your business idea and then how to develop and select lifestyle choices that will ensure your long-term success. It is not a how to guide on building a business as there are plenty of those available. This book is designed to act more like a basic thought guide as you plan your own journey towards becoming and being a sustainable entrepreneur.

Before we continue, I want to clear up a misconception. Many of us define ourselves by what we do for a living, when everything, all human enterprise, comes down to business. Whether you are a butcher, baker, or fashion blogger, you are still ultimately in business first. Perhaps a more productive way of defining ourselves would be to change the way that we introduce ourselves and describe who we are. Instead of defining ourselves by what we do in business, we should focus on the business first and then on what the business does second.

Successful businesses make money providing what customers want and are willing to pay for to receive. There is the secret, if you want to start a business, it is about making money. What your business does to earn that money is secondary to the fact that it is a business first. If that is the case, then we need to focus on developing those business skills needed to ensure your greatest success. As the author of this book, I do not just want to just describe myself as an author. Instead, I am a solutions finder, a personal business coach, college professor of business and entrepreneurship, and a serial entrepreneur who just happens to write books to make all those things more impactful.

Focusing on the business aspect of your business first and then what your business does second helps you put priorities in proper order. If you are a baker, then your response is when someone asks you what you do you be "I own and run a bakery specializing in…" Notice the response? You are setting your mindset as being in the business of baking. The most important thing here is that you focus on the fact that you are in business first and that your business bakes for its customers. This may just seem to be word play, but in reality, it is a powerful tool of self-determination and self-definition. What this does is focuses your thoughts on the critical business functions needed to be successful in your line of business. It helps you, as the entrepreneur, to remember to focus on those things and make the business first decisions that will best improve your business. It helps you to focus on the business of your business first. By doing this, you can set in motion the things that will allow your business to be successful so you can enjoy the passion of whatever your business may focus on.

Many of us enjoy what we do for a living, but we would not do our work without receiving money for our labor. We go to work, start businesses, and sell products to earn money. We want the money to enjoy the lifestyle and financial freedom we dream about and for. If we are not focused on making our business successful, then we might as well just be an employee in someone else's business and not worry about ever being our own boss. If the most important thing to us is baking, or whatever other profession we choose, then we can do that as employees with a lot less responsibility. Of course, that also means a lot less chance for rewards. If, however, the purpose is more than just performing a job, then business ownership and the focus needed is really the key to our success. Business ownership is the vehicle, and the product is the engine that can help drive us to the destination of self-definition and self-determination.

With the ground rules in place, which is starting a business is about making money with the products or services we sell, we can begin to focus on how to be successful. What does it take to make a business successful? First, it takes a desire. You must have the desire to build something that is yours and that you define and refine. Remember, you will define what you do as an entrepreneur, and you should never let *it* define you. You will take your desires, vision, and focus and center them on becoming and being an entrepreneur. Now, before we continue, there seems to be a lot of misconceptions about what it means to be entrepreneurial. While we can in no way cover all those definitions in this book, let us at least set our own definition that will allow us to build a framework to be successful.

The Merriam-Webster Dictionary defines an entrepreneur as "a person who starts a business and is willing to risk loss in order to make money." Not to belabor the point, but it is interesting to note that it did not say someone who is a butcher, baker, or fashion blogger (and yes bloggers can make a business of blogging). It said that an entrepreneur is someone who starts a business with the intention of making money and is willing to take the risks associated with it. What a business does to make money is up to the personal discretion, talents, and demands of the business owner and their customers. One thing the definition does not mention is that an entrepreneur is also a business owner who is willing to reap the benefits that come with business ownership while doing what they enjoy. Let us at least cover a few of those benefits after we discuss the risks of owning your own business.

Lean in a little here. I am going to tell you a little secret. Sometimes businesses fail. Sometimes people lose money when they start a business. Sometimes when people have done all that they can do they do not succeed. They fail and it hurts them financially. In my experience as a professor of entrepreneurship and as a business consultant, the financial hurt is almost never as impactful as the hurt that comes to personal pride. In the end, however, those that do not let failures dictate what they are, get up, dust themselves off, and start anew. They start anew with more experience, knowledge, and understanding of what does not work (or what does not work for them). In many ways the failures become a foundational education which results in long-term success without ever entering a classroom.

Of course, there is the other side of the story. The optimistic vision sometimes can result in outstanding personal and financial outcomes. (We will talk about that particular order in a bit.) When people plan smart, mitigate risk, and understand that they are in business first, they can be very successful. Sometimes they do this even when they have experienced failure. In fact, for most successful entrepreneurs their success is built as much on failure as it is on success. They see their successes as being built not just on the things they have done correctly but on the powerful lessons learned with their failures. Assuming that failure is an option and is part of the risk of being in business for yourself, we must be willing to accept the fear of failure will be present. It is part of dictating and following our own vision for ourselves. This means that fear will not ever really go away. However, instead of letting it paralyze you from action, let it be a motivator. The only real issue left then is whether we accept it and give in or move past it to better things. Entrepreneurs, who maintain the desire for success, go beyond failures to reach their dreams. A few of them are so successful we have a name for them – millionaires.

Who are these millionaires and what does that mean for us striving to get there? About 66% of all millionaires in the United States are self-employed; they make up 20% of workers, and account for two-thirds of all millionaires. Three out of four of those individuals consider themselves to be entrepreneurs. (For a study on this read *The Millionaire Next Door: The Surprising Secrets of America's Wealthy* by Thomas J. Stanley & William D. Danko). If you want to build your own business and consider the risks worth it to be successful, you are by definition, an entrepreneur. As an entrepreneur, you are part of the engine of the economy. With the right kind of planning and preparation, you can address and mitigate most of the risks you are likely to face. However, that does not mean failure is not an option or a possibility. What it means is that you are willing to address those risks and accept that if you do something unique, you will be richly rewarded in defining what your future will be.

The majority of self-made millionaires, those entrepreneurs we want to emulate to be successful, have taken significant risks and failed. As noted, failure in this case was not a curse but a blessing in disguise. Diamonds are not polished in the absence of friction but in its presence and application of friction. Sam Walton, founder of Wal-Mart said, "I believe in always having goals, and always setting them high." Mr. Walton, an exceptional entrepreneur, understood that not all goals are achieved. Without risks, we never achieve anything of lasting value. Knowing what risks are there and working past, over, around, and sometimes through those risks is one of the unique benefits of being an entrepreneur and are worth the effort!

Benefits of Business Ownership

Money: Earning more money is, for most individuals, the main benefit of starting and running their own business. Money is not a bad motivator to start with but tends to lose its sustaining power when a company starts to meet minimum living requirements. For many small business owners, reaching the point where work levels and life levels are in a desired balance are all that they want. In chapters 7 and 9, we will discuss how to balance making money as a component of your whole life. We will discuss how finding a balance in your life is critical no matter what your money aspirations may be.

Being Your Own Boss: The ability to call all the shots is a huge motivator for many entrepreneurs. For individuals with lots of previous work experience, before opening their own business, this is the opportunity to "do things differently" than they have experienced in their careers. For some entrepreneurs, who lack a formal education, it is a way to validate that it does not take a college degree to become successful in business. You can hardly argue this point with successful enterprises run by Bill Gates, Michael Dell, or Richard Branson that proves hard work and on-the-job education (i.e., just doing it) often seems to trump a formal education.

Just a note on education. Many would be entrepreneurs never take action because they do not feel they have the education and skills to be successful. As a college professor, I am convinced of the value of a good education. But I am also of the opinion that some people will simply be successful regardless of education because they learn as they go. While I believe the skills developed through the acquisition of a college education are amazing and can provide practical foundations across a broad spectrum of business domains (accounting, management, human resources, supply chain management, etc.) it does not mean you cannot *earn* that education in another way. In the end, an education alone does not mean you will be successful in business and nor does it mean you will come up with great business ideas. Education is important, but it is not as important in business as hard work.

Let me take just a moment to share a thought that you may ultimately hear from other small business owners as you build your own business. You may, in conversations, hear someone say something like this, "When you work for someone else you only have one boss, when you have your own company, everyone is your boss." But wait, I hear some of you crying foul, "you said starting my own company means I can be the boss." Was I lying? No, not at all. The point these fine business owners are trying to make is that companies must satisfy their customers, or they simply do not make money. Sometimes, therefore, customers will demand a lot from you and your business to ensure you get the sale. However, the business is still yours, the earnings from the business are still yours, and you ultimately have the say in who you choose to do business with. You are after all still the boss of your own destiny and success in your business.

Stay Small or Grow Big if You Want: To grow or not to grow? That is the question. With apologies to Shakespeare, the question is a valid one. For many small business owners, controlling the size of their business is a major issue. They see their business is successful but do not want it to grow beyond a certain level. There are a lot of reasons for keeping a business small, but generally it comes down to life and work balance. If, however, you desire to grow your business beyond certain bounds, you have that option when you are in charge. It is certain that you will experience some growing pains and deal with learning new management techniques along the way, but it is ultimately your business and your choice to grow your business. It is freedom of choice and independence, based on your choices and planning that will allow you to grow your business until you become an entrepreneurial millionaire in your own right.

Tax Benefits: It is well beyond the scope of this book to discuss all the tax benefits of owning your own business. However, there are quite a few and they do make a huge difference in your annual tax bill. This is particularly true for individuals who wish to work a day job and then start a part time company on the side. Keep in mind that as a business owner you are responsible for paying your own taxes, filings, and being in compliance with all local, state, and federal tax regulations. You will need to seek professional advice about taxes to make sure you do not run afoul of the law. This is one of those points where people stop and say, "See that is why I couldn't be self-employed." My response to them is that if I am making more money, I am out of debt (or am getting out of debt quicker), and enjoy being my own boss, why do I care if I pay more taxes? Now, if you are smart you will understand what they do not understand. That when planned correctly, small business owners can actually pay far less personal taxes and have far less tax burdens by a percentage of total income. Why? Because the United States Government understands that small business is the engine of the economy. While tax rates will continue to change depending on which party is in office, tax benefits and savings for small business have remained fairly consistent when measured over time. Again, let me state this so we are clear, this is not an area where gray area is okay. Stay clear of problems and seek ethical professional and competent professional help.

You Get to Invest in Yourself: Being able to invest yourself and your time while doing what you want to full time or even part time is incredibly liberating. That does not mean that running your own company does not come without having to do "the paperwork." What it means is that by and large you get to choose how things are done. You get to set the ground rules for operating your own business and are answerable to yourself as the boss. For some small business owners, focusing on what they do in their business and then paying someone else to do the paperwork is the best possible investment. It leaves them time to be actively involved in the business of their business. Whatever your motivations and methodologies for running your business, being able to run your business, and being able to invest the time in yourself to become a better you are a major benefits.

Start With a Little or No Capital Down: Regardless of how often it is repeated you do not have to have huge amounts of money to start a business. Some very successful companies: Amazon, Whole Foods, Apple, Dell, Disney, Starbucks, and Mattel all started with very little money and are now household names. What made these companies successful was having a clear vision, hard work, and determination. Not every business will be as successful as these examples, but many businesses are sufficiently successful that they become second and third generation companies. The most important capital that a small business owner has are vision, follow through, and the application of sweat equity. Sweat equity, or the time, effort, and hard work put into your business are often undervalued but have the biggest payouts. But just like investing in your retirement account, it needs to be put into a solid performing instrument to reap a benefit.

Some businesses cannot commence without a significant amount of money to begin. Many of these businesses start out with a bang and then fizzle away into obscurity. Perhaps they do so because their business owners are not as invested as much with their sweat equity. Mark Cuban, founder of Broadcast.com and owner of the Dallas Mavericks said, "Only morons start a business on a loan." While it is difficult to determine intellect based on getting a loan or not, it is generally a very poor choice for starting a business. This is especially true when the idea of building a business is to get out of debt or become financially independent. Starting a business with the burden of a loan repayment plan is really an unnecessary condition. Even with good planning, there is not enough assurance the business is going to be successful so don't add that extra weight of a loan you will still be responsible for paying no matter what happens. Start small and build smart at each level and your business will pay for itself over and over again.

The Real Reasons to Own Your Own Home-Based Business

Despite all the benefits of owning your own business, each of us has to come to understand our real motivation and real reasons. Providing a list of the benefits alone is not enough to motivate someone into action. For some, motivation to take the steps into business ownership comes from a desire to meet and make their own destiny for themselves. For others, it is a matter of doing what they want to do on their own terms. These are both valid reasons but do not, generally, have the staying power alone to keep people motivated to move forward. For any action in life, for every human being, it must come down to the internal faith we have in ourselves, and the determination we must become the person we wish to be.

We must have the faith or the belief that we are worth the effort and will produce a positive result for ourselves and our family. What we dream about and what we want to achieve then becomes the primary motivator. It comes down to building a vision for ourselves and then building our business model and objectives around a personal mission statement. The vision of making more money is then tempered by the vision of the individual we are and will become in the process. There are enough morally derelict individuals with money in the world; we certainly do not need to add ourselves into the mix. What must motivate each of us is a personal mission statement of what we stand for and what we will stand against in our lives and the businesses we start and run.

As noted earlier in the chapter, the personal outcomes in owning a business may be far more important to you than making millions of dollars. So, let us cut right to the point. Most small businesses will not result in making millionaires out of their owners. In some cases, making money in your business may not even be the motivation for starting a business. What if what you want to do is start a non-profit organization that focuses on developing and teaching life skills to inner-city or rural single mothers? Guess what? Your rewards may be mostly focused on the personal satisfaction in creating something on your own just as much as it is for the for-profit business entrepreneur. In the end, many of the skill sets, tools, and practical support skills we will discuss in this book still apply. As an entrepreneur creating, leading, and growing a non-profit business you will still be in business and many of the same approaches provided in this book will help and serve you as you serve those who need your support.

Developing a Personal Mission Statement

Developing a personal mission statement is akin to setting the bylaws under which you will make your decisions and succeed in your business. Your personal mission statement does not need to be complicated; in fact, it is best if it based on simple statements. Your personal mission statement should reflect, at its core, the things that are most important to you. These things will include what you want to represent, what you believe, what you want to be, and the qualities of your character.

Your personal mission statement is an extension of how you think and should be laid out in the best manner, so you can read it regularly. My personal mission statement is linearly laid out because I like order and seek to have order in what I do. Your mission statement must be personal, reflect your personality. It may simply be a list of one-word affirmations. Your mission statement does not have to mirror mine in any way, but I have included elements of my own personal mission statement as a sample.

1. Gain knowledge and communicate daily to grow my personal relationship with God.
2. Be the best husband I can be and never stop courting my bride who is the love of my life.
3. Always be the dad and sometimes the friend my children need.
4. Become a key entrepreneurial advocate for improving people who support and sustain themselves and others in their families and communities.
5. Continue to learn and develop new skills regularly through regular reading, research, and taking classes so I can better communicate with diverse and interesting people.
6. Educate those who desire liberty through the attainment of self-reliance while I enhance my own liberty and self-reliance.
7. Maintain the highest moral and ethical standards in all I do even if others deride my actions.
   a. Be willing to forgive myself and try harder when I fall short of my own personal expectations.

8. Exercise regularly and participate in activities that enhance my physical, mental, and spiritual health and well-being.

As you set your goals and start your business, you should refer to your personal mission statement to see how you are measuring up to your own ideals. You will find that as you move forward and become more successful, your mission statement will provide the guiding principles for how you interact with others and for the kind of individual you are and will become. Take the time now to stop and draft your own mission statement.

I Want to Start My Own Business, What Should I Do?

Once you have developed your personal mission statement, you are ready to move onto the next step of starting your business; figuring out what your business will do. So, what business is best for you? That really depends on you and what you want to achieve. In some ways, it also depends on what skills you have or can develop (we will be discussing skills development more in Chapter 8). Finding a business idea is generally simple but may take some time to define fully. The best way to define your business options is to answer some basic questions. Below, you will find a list of questions that will help you come up with some business ideas. It is not an exhaustive list and is only designed to help you brainstorm some ideas and then to narrow those ideas down to some potential business candidates.

1. What training, skills, and education do I have? Can I use them in creating a business?
2. In using my training, skills, or education, are there areas of service or products that are not currently being offered?
3. Can I make that product or provide that service?
4. What options do I have to produce product or provide the service I have identified?

5. If I have no capital to start the company, can I start it as a part-time microbusiness with little or no money?

6. Who is unserved, underserved, or forgotten by existing service or product providers and how can I reach them?

7. Who would be my primary customer base? Who would be my secondary customer base?

8. How can I communicate with and market my products or services to my primary and secondary customers?

9. How can I develop relationships with my primary and secondary customers that will get them interested in my company's products?

10. How can I get my customers to spread the word about what I provide so my sales and my business can grow?

11. How will I get paid and how will I charge for my products?

12. Am I excited about offering my product or service? Will I still enjoy working on this in 5 years?

13. Will this business be in line with my personal mission statement?

Once you have come up with your potential business candidate ideas, you will need to do some homework to see if your ideas are really viable for a business. What people generally find is that their ideas are not as original as they thought, and they need to refine the business ideas further. Once you have solidified your ideal candidate down to a solid business concept you will have a solid foundation to build on. (Do not be surprised if there is more than one. However, it is best to focus on one business idea at a time.) Then, it is time to set the things in motion to create a business plan. Despite the fact there are a myriad of books and courses available to help you write a multipage business plan, most small home-based businesses or microbusiness do not need anything that complex. A one-page business plan is all you really need to get started. Your one-page business plan should include the following information:

1. What is the mission of your business? (What are you going to do?)

2. What is the vision of your business? (How will you go about fulfilling your mission and with what operating principles?)

3. What do you want to accomplish? (Provide some basic goals and at least two milestones towards those goals. For this plan, think in terms of goals for 6 months, 12 months, and 24 months.)

4. What strategies are you setting in place to accomplish the goals set for yourself? (This should include a basic marketing strategy, sales strategy, and a customer engagement strategy.)

5. What is your basic action plan towards your milestones and goals? (This should be most of the page as it will provide a high-level plan of what you need to do to be successful in your business.)

Of course, the next task is to take the first step and get started. Make your business goals a reality by taking action. While you are not alone in this process of starting your business, you may have to manage many of the steps by yourself. But there are several good resources to help answer your questions. With a little research on the internet, you can find a local business development group and the Small Business Administration (SBA) closest to you. Much of the assistance you get from these groups is free, and they often sponsor networking groups that meet regularly and include other local business entrepreneurs. Use these resources to make sure you meet all the legal licensing and tax obligations within your community. Nothing kills the excitement of a growing business faster than to hit the brick wall of legal or tax problems.

Chapter 2: Money Management

Once you have set all your actions in motion and your business becomes a success, the need for practical money management will become increasingly important. I would say it was important before then, but it becomes more important. While no business will succeed for long with bills to pay and no cash flow to pay them, there is something far more dangerous. That is the habit that some business owners get into of paying themselves too early and too much. This condition is much like a virus. It starts out as with a simple rationalization of, "Hey, I made some money; I should be able to spend it." It begins with small things and soon it grows until you are fully infected. This infection is the same disease that gets people in debt to begin with. So, prepare yourself and your way of thinking early to avoid this problem. An ounce of prevention is well worth the effort, believe me. Your business is an investment in today and the future, and you need to inoculate yourself early. To inoculate yourself, requires you to first build a cash reserve and then practice strong money management skills. With time, you will have built up a resistance to debt through stable and sustainable wealth. There will be a time to buy what you want with cash and not credit. If you have created within yourself the discipline to know when to hold and when to spend, you will create a powerful skill set to improve not only your business but your personal finances as well.

Having a cash reserve could be the difference between getting or losing that next big customer or job in your business; the customer or job that will notch your business up one level. If business owners learn a few simple money management rules early, they will be prepared for the ups and downs that are inevitable in every business. Liquid capital, or cash available, is an incredibly powerful tool that gives you options. It allows individuals and companies to have the greatest flexibility to make choices.

Let us use an example to illustrate this point: Sarah and Steve own a part time catering business. They have a clear mission statement, and they have built a profitable small company. They have been in business for a couple of years, and they love what they do as it allows them to work together as husband and wife. After a while, however, they forget the reason they started the business, which was to get out of debt. They begin to raise their lifestyle to meet their new income level. As a reward for their hard work, they decide to take a vacation to Hawaii. They feel they have earned this as a reward for their hard work and planning. However, to afford the vacation they pay themselves a bonus and dip into the cash reserves of the business. The problem is that they leave their business with little or no reserve capital. They go on vacation and have a great time.

Once they get back from their vacation, Beth, who is about to get married in four weeks, calls and says she wants Sarah and Steve to cater her wedding reception. To ensure this job and customer, Beth wants to taste some meal samples. Beth also wants Sarah and Steve to take care of managing the rental of all the dinnerware, tables, and tablecloths which is something they have wanted to do anyway. As an added bonus, Beth tells Sarah and Steve that she has three other friends who are getting married in the next six months, and they are going to use their services if all things go well.

Sarah and Steve are in a bind here. They have spent all their reserve cash and are left with very few options. This is where small business owners make the biggest mistakes. They try to bluff their way out of the situation. They hide the fact they do not have money to purchase supplies for food samples. They do the next best thing they can think of, they charge the expenses to a credit card. All the sudden, they have created a situation of additional stress. They now have no money in the bank, a credit card bill to pay, and no certainty that Beth is going to hire them. Simply maintaining a cash reserve may not have covered all the expenses but would likely have covered most. As the company matures and develops, they can rely exclusively on funding growth opportunities without further debt. Business schools teach that strategic business debt is a great business tool and to a point that is correct. However, being a debt-free business with cash reserves gives you freedom, choices, and flexibility without being accountable to creditors.

Owning a business can be incredibly rewarding, but it comes with its own natural stresses. Adding the stress of poor money management need not be one of them. Applying some sound money management principles can make all the difference in reducing undue stress. It can help to ensure you are able to succeed whether an opportunity like one Beth proposes works out or not. In the next few pages, we are going to talk about some practices that will help grow your business, so you can attain financial independence from your own business.

Open a Separate Bank Account for Your Business: This is personally my first small business money management rule. It may be one of the most important. It helps to remind business owners that the money in that account belongs first to the business. You pay yourself from this account and you deposit payments from your customers into this account. If you are starting out with no capital startup, you can use your own bank account to begin with. However, as quickly as possible, setup a separate account. Keep in mind that you need to have a clear differentiation between you and the business. You are not your business, and your business is not you, even if you are a one-person business. By having a separate bank account, you are reminding yourself of this fact. As a reminder, you need to maintain the receipts and payments from this business separate from your personal bills and statements.

Create and use a Personal and a Business Budget: For some reason in our modern world, we have forgotten budgeting as a critical life skill our forebears understood and lived by. According to the United States Bureau of Labor, we have drastically changed the way we spend money in this country. The fact is we have created a culture of debt that lessens our personal and business options and keeps us locked into our bad decisions. If we take a moment to look just at our personal budgets and spending habits, it is clear we have a personal, community, state, and national problem. We are addicted to debt, and we are not saving for a rainy day. Rainy days always come.

In 1900, families spent 80% of their family budget on food, housing, and clothes. In 1950, families spent 70% of their budget on food, housing, and clothes. In 2021, families spent 68.5% of their income on the same three items. So why have we gotten so in debt when it is clear that the cost of feeding, housing, and clothing ourselves has been reduced as a percentage of our household spending? Is it healthcare? Well, yes, that is part of it. However, most of those costs are lost in our other spending that may or may not be necessary. As of early 2024 the average monthly cost of food is up 13%, housing is up 7%, and clothing and services is up 11%. Many families are turning to credit to cover increased expenses and stagnant wage growth. This simply solidifies the need for earning more so that budgeting is not a zero or negative personal proposition.

There are a couple of additional costs that are high that we should consider, but even with these taken into consideration and budgeted for with practicality can be controlled. The first is the cost of transportation. Of course, this cost is, to a great deal, self-inflicted. Many of us work in large cities and commute to and from work daily. This cost is one that many, post COVID pandemic, realized they did not have to need to have. This was because remote work became the solution for many during the pandemic. In reality, the pandemic simply expedited a change that was already an emerging work trend. Work from home, if it is a possibility for you, may be one option in helping to reduce your personal transportation expenses thus helping your budgeting efforts.

Healthcare costs are of course another high budgeting item. Healthcare is expensive and government manipulation of healthcare does not help. We are not likely to see a nationalized healthcare system in the United States, so healthcare costs will continue to be a portion of your budget and you need to get used to it. The truth is, however, that most of us could reduce our healthcare costs if we would change our own eating and exercise patterns. We will talk a little more about that later in the book and how these relate to sustainable entrepreneurship. You may not yet see the connection, but it is there.

In the end, the real ailment we have in government, in companies, and in our homes is we are addicted to debt. We must break this cycle and the best place to do that is one person and family at a time. We do that by producing and rebuilding our economy in the way it was built to begin with. We do this by free enterprise and personal debt reduction. Entrepreneurship and personal business ownership are part of the answer. Once we address our own personal debt cycle and budget to live within our means and increase our earnings, we will be better able to change our local, state, and national debt issues. When individuals and families begin to see themselves as the solution to addressing their own needs, they will be less inclined to look to the government to solve their financial problems. By extension they will then vote for those who will demand debt reduction at the local, state, and national level. They will do this so that taxes go to support those things defined by the US Constitution and not by personal pet projects of senators and representatives. People who are financially secure in supporting themselves will have less need to seek support from government systems. Those government systems will then be there just to address the needs of those most in need and those veterans whose efforts ensured our liberties continue. Of course, that is not the purpose of this book, but you can quickly see the connections are myriad and breaking the debt cycle is a good thing for more than just you and your family. We will discuss personal debt reduction more in a moment.

I will be the first to tell you that I used to hate using a written budget. I had to force myself to stick to the budget and I felt like, for most people, it is the same. Plus, I thought it was unrealistic to use a rigid budget because, 'what if I change my mind and I want to spend my money in a different way than planned?' Do you see the problem there? The problem is that I was thinking about a budget as controlling me verses me controlling my money so in the future I could have the liberty and freedom to live differently.

A personal budget and a business budget need to be thought of in a different way. We need to move beyond the now moment and think about our long-term vision for ourselves and for the company we want to create. We must move beyond forcing ourselves to use a written budget only when we are trying to save for something that is a need or want. We must move to budgeting to create a life for ourselves that is not limited by the confines of personal debt and plan for personal and business growth. Does that mean it is easy? No, of course not. However, it gets easier with time, just like everything else. Repeated efforts focused on daily, weekly, monthly, and annual budgeting are critical in taking your mission statement and vision statement and turning them into a lived reality.

Telling you how to budget is not the purpose of this chapter or this book. You must find the budgeting process that works for you and which you can be faithful in using. In the end, how you budget is not nearly as important as that you budget and account for every earned and spent penny. As long as we stay below that set dollar amount, and save a little for a rainy day, you are on the way to becoming a budgeting hero. After all, the person who can always support you when you have financial hiccups is for sure a hero. You should be the hero in your own story. Not only is it responsible, but it is also really cool, as well.

For your business we need to talk about how budgeting and how you run your business can make all the difference in avoiding the debt trap and being the financial hero in your own business, as well. The ideas presented below are those gained from years of personal entrepreneurship and business consulting with other entrepreneurs. How you choose to use this information is, like the rest of this book, up to you. My word of caution is do not dismiss these ideas as simplistic. They may be simple, but they are powerful.

Run a Cash Business: If consumer debt is a problem for you when starting your business, then you need to sever the debt habit and learn to deal in cash. Money talks and when you can, you should always use cash. A debit card that is tied to a bank account is a great way to still use plastic if you have no other choice. However, use caution in your own business when it comes to receiving credit card payments too early in your business. Accepting payment card payments (credit and debit card), is important but it may not be critical to start your business.

Many new business owners are shocked when they find out that they are charged a fee for every time a customer uses a credit card or debit. It may not seem like a lot per transaction, but over the course of a year even at a 2% per transaction fee, you will be paying a lot for the privilege of letting your customers use credit cards. In many businesses, you can simply ask your customers to pay in cash (or by check if you have no other choice). If you have a customer that insists on paying by credit card, then use a credit card swipe service on your mobile phone as an option and adjust your product or service pricing to compensate for the transaction fees.

I have found in my businesses that if I must take credit cards for anything, I have people make a payment to my PayPal account. If you explain the cost of credit card transactions to your customers, most of them are happy to save you money. If you find ways to pass on the savings in some way to them, it is a win-win. Running your business this way forces you to look at what you are making and what you are spending. If you practice some early credit discipline and think about how much it takes to earn every dollar, you will find you spend less and save more.

You Earned the Money, Now Hold on To It: At least, a portion of everything you make in your business needs to be reinvested back into the business or held in cash reserves. I would love to give you some exact percentages, but that really depends on the nature of your business and what you need to cover expenses. It should also include money needed for developing a cash fund for surprise opportunities and emergencies. In the early stages of growing your business, it makes a lot of sense to roll everything back into the business if you can. However, if you are going to take money early, always error on the side of caution; a general rule is to never take more than 50% out of your net earnings. This will give you the ability to meet most any unforeseen expenses. When it comes time to pay yourself, write a check to yourself. I personally avoid transferring money into my personal account just to avoid combining the two different account purposes in my own thinking. If I see the business bank account as not connected to my personal accounts, I am less likely to overspend and more likely to stay within my defined budget in my company (and personally). As an added benefit, this always gives me a paper trail to follow for accounting purposes.

Avoid Giving Customers Unnecessary Credit: One of the dangers of trying to make a sale when you are starting a new business is allowing customers to pay you on credit. As a new business, avoid this any way you can. While in some industries, this is a custom, in small businesses it should be avoided as much as possible. If you have no choice, there are ways to work around not extending full credit, but they require a level of finesse and persuasion. Avoid performing a service or providing a product unless you receive payment at the time of or before delivery. Remember, the whole point of your business is to diminish and avoid debt; whether it is yours or customer credit which is just debt owed to you. In other words, don't be an enabler for continuing the debt cycle in others. Keep in mind, that as a small business owner, it is generally cost prohibitive for you to run credit checks on your customers. It can be done, but it is not worth the costs to your bottom line. Just keep this idea in mind, if you are extending credit, you have likely just created more of a debt problem for yourself. While your business is new and small, focus on sales to customers that are going to provide prompt payment with each transaction. As your small company matures and you have built a reserve, you can then go back and address credit options, if you must.

Live Within Your Means: While this may sound a bit repetitive, do not let yourself fall into the *spend more because you make more* trap. Make your budget and live within that budget. Remember, conservative budgeting and spending less than you earn is the surest way to ensure your hard-earned wealth is lasting. This is true personally and for your business. Companies that operate within their means and are conservative in their spending may grow slower at times, but they grow with enough capital resources to have a solid foundation. They can ride out the inevitable up and down cycles of sales that small businesses often deal with. Benjamin Franklin summed this up very well, "When you run in debt; you give to another power over your liberty." Individual freedom and wealth earned while building your own destiny and staying out of debt are keys to becoming a sustainable entrepreneur.

Individuals that are focused on get rich quick schemes often lose what they make faster than they earned it. If you need proof of this, just look at the history of lottery winners in the United States. The researchers in a study conducted by Vanderbilt University, the University of Kentucky, and the University of Pittsburgh found nearly 70% percent of lottery winners who had won between $50,000 and $100,000 were broke within 7 years. That may not be a lot of money, but it is easy to see that the individuals who have not developed the talent, tools, and skills to spend less even when they make more cannot hold on to what they have. Said another way, people do not prosper with handouts and when on the public dole. People and countries prosper and maintain their wealth when they learn how to earn and save from their own labors.

Let us pause for a moment and consider a life lesson. It is one I hope you will pass on to your children and those with whom you serve (we will talk about this more in Chapter 7). What would be better, to win a million dollars and lose it or to earn a million dollars and lose it? Now some of you are saying neither one, in both cases I am without the money at the end of the deal. But are you really worse off? If you *win* the money and lose it, chances are you will not win more. However, if you have done your homework, worked hard, built a business, and have *earned* a million dollars, and lose it, you still have something of value. You will have the knowledge and the ability to do it again and again. I will take the earned skills and knowledge every time.

Living within your means may not keep you from ever losing what you make. What it will do is provide you with the strongest possible skillset to keep building your wealth no matter what happens. Even if you hit rock bottom and had to start over again you will know what you need to do to get back to where you have been. The person who does not learn how to earn does not know how to earn when the well runs dry. The life lesson here is to leave gambling and lottery by the wayside and invest in yourself and your money education.

Always Roll a Percentage of Your Earnings Back into Wealth Building and Education: The most important investment in wealth building is a three-part approach. First, it may sound counterintuitive to give the first 10% away, but the first 10% should be given to God, charity, or a worthy cause. We will talk about why this is important in

Chapter 9. For the moment, suffice it to say that a donation to a higher cause helps us to remain humble and opens us up to thinking about money as a tool and nothing more. Besides, humility is important. There is nothing worse than a haughty rich person. Sure, we all want to be debt free and at liberty from the burdens that come with it. However, we do not want to become insufferable and lose ourselves in the process. Dale Carnegie said it best, "Success is getting what you want. Happiness is wanting what you get." The loss of your good friends and family along the way is an unacceptable price to pay for acquiring wealth.

Second, take the time to build a library and read books on success, business leadership, and self-development. Avoid fad business books which are mostly psychobabble. All they will do is poison your mind and keep you from the path of success. Study those individuals who are successful in both improving personal and business relationships. Zig Ziglar had a great summation of this concept, "Rich people have small TVs and big libraries, and poor people have small libraries and big TVs." Ditch the distractions, sit down every day, and take time to read about those people you wish to emulate. Personally, I read for an hour before I go to bed each night. I concentrate part of my reading time on improving my spirituality and the other part on something that interests and inspires me. Each morning I take a few minutes for reading scriptures before I start my day to set my focus on what is really important to me. These practices allow me to finish a significant number of books each month. Spending this dedicated time, means I get to sit at a table and learn from successful people every day. Reading is a habit that successful people develop to educate themselves. Invest in books and then read regularly. Fancy books on a bookshelf may look nice but will not help you improve in anyway. If you cannot afford buying physical books, consider getting a tablet as eBooks are generally less expensive to buy or even "check out" with services like Amazon Prime. If you cannot afford the eBook option, remember that the public library is always a great option. Check out a book and learn for free.

Finally, as soon as you can, set aside a little of your business earnings and attend seminars and forums. Attend those events that focus on personal development, sales, and marketing. You do not have to spend a lot of money to do this. In fact, many cities and metropolitan areas have networking groups and professional associations that you can join or take part in as a guest. These groups will often have free or inexpensive seminars that you can get invited to attend. I have found that these organizations are often willing to give you an annual membership at a discount or free if you are willing to participate as a speaker. This is a great way to network as well as educate potential clients about what your company has to offer.

Budget and Eliminate Your Debt: The Motley Fool, a financial and investment company, presented the following sobering statistics for the year 2023. The average household credit household debt was $103,358. The average mortgage debt was $241,815. Add to that the average of $37,338 in student loans according to Education Data Initiative. Yes, you read that right, the average US household with a home loan and student debt has $382,511 of debt hanging over their heads. We buy on credit outside of what we really have today, sometimes at astronomical interest rates. Setting up a budget and living within that budget is critical to your personal and business success. More than that, it is critical if you want to get out of debt. Make a budget and include a plan for getting out of debt and then stick to it. As you earn more money in your business, make sure you are using it to get free of the burden and stress of your debt. Debt free people may not always be millionaires, but they might as well be if everything they earn is going towards wealth building instead of towards bills. I highly recommend further reading on your part. I highly recommend *The Total Money Makeover: A Proven Plan for Financial Fitness Look* by Dave Ramsey. His work focuses on tried-and-true principles of debt reduction and is a great go to reference in your business library. It is not the only approach but is a solid place to begin your efforts.

Rent to Get Out of Debt: You do not need to own your own home. For many people who are deeply in debt, owning a home is a significant liability. Unless you have a great deal of equity in your home or own your home outright, renting is a logical option for someone starting a business. Despite what many of us have been taught to believe, a house is not an asset. It will always cost you money and it isn't making you any money. Robert Kiyosaki explained this very succinctly in his book *Rich Dad Poor Dad*. If you are paying a mortgage, especially one that is honestly out of your budget, then renting is a great option for getting out of debt. If you own your own home, you are responsible for all the upkeep and repairs. Some of those repairs can be very expensive and will wreck your budget. When you rent, you will probably cover the costs of lawn care, but other upkeep and repairs are your landlord's responsibility. That takes the burden off you so you can concentrate on building your own business. Of course, in the current market of late 2023 the cost of renting may actually be more expensive than buying a home. In the end, seek professional financial advice for the best option for your family.

There is one caveat to renting and starting a business. If you are going to run your business from the home you are renting, you will need to have the approval of your landlord. He or she is responsible for making sure you are not violating any laws that would get either of you into legal trouble. For most internet businesses, this is not usually a huge deal if you are not actively moving products or producing product from your home. If, however, you decide to have a service company where you may have a truck or trailer in front of your house, then that is something else altogether. Learn the laws, know the laws, and keep yourself out of trouble. Legal advice from qualified professionals, even at some cost, is better than paying painful fees and penalties that can ruin your business.

Financial Literacy is a Lifelong Quest

Financial literacy is, unfortunately, one of the most overlooked aspects of education of us and our children. Unfortunately, many entrepreneurs are stopped cold in pursuit of their dreams by poor money management skills. If your intention is to build a business so that you can attain financial independence, you are going to have to do more than just budget money. You are going to have to learn how money works and how it can be a tool for creating security and greater wealth. The problem is that there are tons of people out there who are willing to help you part with your hard-earned money, so they can sell you their investment scheme. While an in-depth discussion about investment options is beyond the scope of this book, I will at least touch on a couple of things to consider.

Cash is King: There is nothing wrong with using cash for as many transactions as possible. If you must use plastic for your purchases, make sure it is a debit card attached to a bank account. Purchasing with cash makes it easier to stick with your budget. What you want to do is develop a habit of carrying cash in your wallet or purse. One close friend said that he knew he was becoming successful when he always had a $100 bill in his wallet. When he was tempted to spend it or go beyond his budget, he would think about that $100 bill and what he had to do to earn it. He said it helped him to keep on track and stick with his goals. He said after a while $100 was not enough to motivate him anymore so he bumped it up to $500 at all times. You do not need to carry around a bunch of cash all the time. However, you do need to find a way to keep yourself on track and within your budget. As a final note, I have found if I have cash in hand, I can often bargain for items I am purchasing. Credit will buy you things, but you will pay for it forever; cash is a onetime transaction and will help to keep buying interest free.

Retirement Savings Can be Harmful: Retirement planning and investments are important but can be harmful if not thought out logically. If you are in debt up to your eyeballs and you are socking away 15% of your annual earnings what good is that? Not much at all. Individuals who have invested in retirement plans who must turn right around and pay off all their outstanding debts when they retire are no better off than they were before. They have no wealth and now have no income to support themselves. Where do they end up? In poor paying part time jobs that belittle the hard work they spent their life doing. I am not saying that being a discount store greeter is a bad thing. It is just not for me, and I suspect does not meet your definition of being financially free in your older years.

If that person saved a little less and started and built a business, they would be able to change the whole dynamic of their life. Imagine if you built your business and then sold it for a tidy profit. You could then have your money work for you. It could be put into an investment that would have lasting value. It could continue to pay for you to enjoy your retirement to the fullest. You would be free to make choices versus having your circumstances dictate your lifestyle. Of course, if you love what you do and it makes you money, you may decide you do not ever want to retire because you are having too much fun doing what you love to do while you are making money.

Teach Your Kids Early and Often: Teaching our children as we learn is nothing new for us as parents. As you learn and develop your own financial literacy, pass it on to your children. It is amazing how many young people do not understand simple interest, proper use of credit cards, or how to balance a checkbook. Do not let the mistakes that got you into debt be repeated for another generation. As you learn how to better manage your money, you should be passing it on to your children and grandchildren.

Developing money management skills is a lifetime endeavor. Even when we have learned one principle, we will find that there is still more to learn. How you manage your money when you are earning an extra $100 dollars a week, and what you need to do when earning a $1,000 a week are not the same. For most of us, the beginning of our business earning goes into reducing and paying off our debts. Once we have paid off those debts, we must use strategies to hold onto and use our money wisely. In the next chapter, we are going to talk about how we not only use money more wisely but how thrifty living can help us save more of what we earn.

Chapter 3: Thrift

You have done your homework, started your own business, and it is making money. Happily, it is making the kind of money you have been dreaming about. Rightfully so, you consider yourself a success. You are applying practical money management and rolling sufficient money back into your business just in case something happens. You are even saving some personal money for personal emergencies. Then you hit this chapter about thrift. Why in the world would I bring the topic of thrift into the conversation? After all, the whole point of your business is to get you out of debt by building a business, so you can buy what you want when you want. If your business is successful, then you should be able to spend your earnings however you want – right? Yes, you can, but it is probably not the best policy. Thrift is the sister of good money management and should be the policy of every sustainable entrepreneur.

Practicing thrifty living principles is not just for people who lived through the Great Depression or the Great Recession. It needs to be the rallying call of those who have lived through great debt and the hard times that come with it. Living thrifty is a manifestation that we are committed to a lifestyle of freedom based on personal values and strong money management skills. It demonstrates we know where we have been and that we will use our money wisely, so we never return. We do not want to be in the position of having it all and then losing it. It is no fun being unemployed, especially if you must fire yourself from your own business.

Let us take a minute a talk a little about unemployment, as it is an important concept for business owners to understand. Government claims that unemployment numbers have dropped never tell the whole story about the economy. As aggregated data, they do not show us the individual tragedies and challenges. They also do not generally tell us why people are unemployed. The number one issue is that our economy is changing, and our government is still acting as if it was in yesterdays or yesteryears economy. Politicians in both parties, who have never been small business owners, do not understand and neither do many American citizens that our economy is dynamic and ever changing. Just for the record, this is not necessarily a bad thing. As a would-be entrepreneur it is your chance to see and capitalize those changes to create a business.

The working population of the United States used to be able to count on rapid expansion and growth of our economy through manufacturing ramp ups. We could do this because our economy was manufacturing based. When consumers felt confident, they purchased more manufactured products and economic downturns would end as a result. Companies that manufactured products hired more people and those people, with new incomes could in turn, buy more products. It was a great system and worked amazingly well. However, those days are gone.

The manufacturing infrastructure that got us out of downturns and recessions simply does not exist anymore in the United States, or at least to the same degree it did in the past. We could lament and argue all day if that is a good or bad thing, but it would not change the fact that it is currently a fact of life. Manufacturing is no longer the backbone of our economy. It could be again and should be again, but that will take at least a decade of reshoring and is really beyond the scope of this book. The result of this change is people who could once count on jumping to another company to find manufacturing jobs are not able to find those positions. They cannot now because those positions do not exist. In some cases, these people have simply given up their search for a job entirely. They stay on unemployment for as long as they can and then finally give up their search altogether. At that point, the government no longer counts them on the roles of the unemployed. For those who refuse to give up, the result of the new economy means they are forced to take part time jobs or multiple part time jobs. These jobs are generally positions where they are significantly underpaid and underemployed. Circumstances have dictated their new lifestyles versus people dictating their own lifestyles. Their lives would likely have been very different if they had been owners of a small business and practiced thrift. They would have had the option to ramp up their small business into a full-time endeavor and could have lived within their means. This is not to say this is the case for every small business owner, but it is a distinct possibility for many of them.

Save It and Use It Wisely: I am sure some of you are asking what in the world does this have to do starting my business? So, let me get to the point. If you raise your lifestyle to meet your income, then you create a situation where major, and sometimes minor, economic changes can have a devastating effect. There will always be seasonal dips in sales; that is only part of the issue. The other part is that people live at the level of their income with no buffer and have developed no skills to reduce their cost of living. They fail to understand that practicing a thrifty lifestyle, at any income, will help them cope when changes and downturns occur. As you practice thrift, you will be able to readjust your personal life, your business focus, services, and products to meet economic changes. If you live exactly at a level equal to your earnings, you will not have the flexibility to meet those dips and changes. If you are living on less than you make, have a rainy-day fund, and are practicing thrifty living, you will be better able to change your course, use your reserves, and ensure long-term success in life and your business.

Practicing thrift will help you to use your resources wisely. You will be able make the minor adjustments needed to your lifestyle until you are able to retool your business with new products and services. Like it or not, how you live outside of your business can have a huge impact on the decisions make inside your business. Practicing a thrifty lifestyle will reduce some of the outside stress, so you can focus your business decisions on those things that will keep you moving forward and profitable.

Thrift is about watching what you spend your money on, and how you make your money work for you. It is about changing the way you think about money. Ask yourself now what is your attitude about money? Most people will say that they love to make money and would love to be out of debt. They would be willing to change the way they handle and use money. Can you say this about yourself? If you see a penny on the ground, will you stop and pick it up? Someone who understands the value of money will. Just ask someone who lived through the Great Depression or long-time unemployment without a check.

Let me pause to share a quick story from when I was 16 years old. I was an Air Force brat, and my family moved every three to four years. If you consider the hops to different houses in the same general area, we actually moved more than that. I have always loved to have fun and to see what people would do if something strange happened. I believe with a camera I could have been a YouTube success for my hijinks, but alas, I am too old for that. Nonetheless, armed with a zip top bag full of pennies with my friends, we headed to the local mall. Being the joker

I have always been, it struck me as funny to see what would happen if we dropped a handful of pennies from the second-floor railing to the first floor below. After making sure the coast was clear and that we would not hit anyone with our dropped coins, we began our experiment. We dropped two handfuls of pennies from the second floor. They made a wonderful sound on the floor below. And other than having people look at us and tell us we were being dumb; everyone left the pennies alone and went about their business. On the third handful of pennies, something different happened. I let go of the pennies and they hit the ground, and a customer in one of the first level stores came out into the common area and began to pick the pennies up. As teenagers, this made us all laugh. That was until she said, "You kids don't know what these pennies are worth. Wait until you have to work for them or don't have anything, and you will regret being so foolish." Fast forward 10 years, when I found myself with a small family and broke. That memory rushed back to hit me hard. That amazing woman taught me a lesson that it took 10 years for me to learn – every penny is worth saving.

Being thrifty is not the absence of buying things you want. It is about delayed gratification, creative buying, and making do when what you have is good enough. It is not necessarily having a love of money but having an understanding that money is a tool. It is about loving the freedom that money can afford you, so you can focus on the things that mean the most to you. Even if that is having one penny above zero when you are debt free.

Money cannot buy happiness, but it can pay for an inexpensive family vacation camping in tents by the local lake for a week. Once there, you can build great memories with your family. Best of all, it is the kind of vacation you will not be paying on for months to come. It means finding ways in your business and your personal life to reduce your expenses, so you can live life to the fullest. Living life to the fullest is not done by how much money you have and spend, it is about doing the things that build memories and will have a lasting impression on your own mind and that of your children. No matter how much you pay to take your 18-month-old to Disneyland, she will not remember it. Take her to the beach or on inexpensive family vacations where you do cheap or free silly things together, and you will imprint in her mind her personal value, and it does not come with a price tag. You can do a lot of free things and stretch your pennies for all they are worth. You will not be throwing your pennies from the second floor with no real benefit. You may not be driving a brand-new Porsche, but you may be driving a Nissan van that is completely yours without a monthly bill. Which would you rather have? I will take the Nissan van debt free any day of the week.

Reduce, Recycle, and Reuse: This is more than protecting the environment and natural resources. When we talk about reduce, recycle, and reuse as a lifestyle and business strategy, it is a means of coming up with products and services that have longevity and are sustainable. One approach is to create products that can be created once and resold multiple times. As we discussed before, we have generally moved away from a manufacturing economy. We have become an information and service economy. While we cannot always perform services once and sell it multiple times, we can certainly do so with information. A book is a great example of this concept in action. The author only needs to write the book once but will be able to sell copies to multiple people. Each person pays for the book individually, yet the author only writes the book once. Despite the dream of one book making you rich, it just does not happen enough to be a practical dream. Instead, your reusable product, your book, can sell multiple times and can be the way to open the door for other products and services; it is a great way to practice reduce, recycle, and reuse to generate a profit.

Now, the other part of reduce, recycle, and reuse is of course founded in its environmental roots. As you are practicing principles of thrift, keep in mind there are some great ways to use your money wisely and be environmentally conscience. This is not because you believe in global warming, global cooling, or climate change. I have never met a person who was mindful of their resources (money or otherwise) who was not a conservationist at heart. In this mindset the reasons are really about economics but are generally ecologically sound. One economical and simple way to reduce waste is to pay as many of your business and personal bills online as you can or feel comfortable with. Most utilities are more than happy to have you pay online as it makes their companies more environmentally conscience and requires less paperwork. In the end, you are saving on stamps, checks, and a run to the mailbox.

Another way to save money is to plan your car trips. Having to gas up the car because of a bunch of separate trips and errand-running is a major budget killer. Most people do not even know how much they spend on gas making quick runs to the store, quick mart, gym, etc. A simple rule for reducing automobile costs is to keep a list of tasks and combine your trips to different stores and for errands into a one-time outing. Keep your list on your smart phone and you will not risk forgetting what needs to be done, and you will be more likely to stick to your budget.

Finally, reuse scrap paper from your business. One great method for reusing printer paper is to use the blank back side of the page. You can save this paper and stack blank sides up with about 25 sheets and staple along the long edge. Then cut the stapled stack in half (in the middle along the long side of the paper) with a pair of scissors. You will be left with two 5½ X 8½ inch notepads. These recycled paper notepads are great for keeping notes with customers while on the phone.

There are tons of ways to reduce, recycle, and reuse. We certainly cannot cover every single one in this book. Remember, the purpose is not so much to save a tree, although that is a nice benefit and who does not like beautiful trees? The purpose of this is to be mindful of how much each penny costs us. If we treat each penny we earn as a prized gift granted by grateful customers who believe in us, our products, and our services, then we will use our money wisely.

Use it Up, Wear it Out, Make It Do, or Do Without: This is perhaps the greatest saying when it comes to thrift. It sets the standard for how to use what you already own and not go farther in debt. Some simple rules can apply to help you spend your hard-earned money in the best way possible. Use it up means that we use something until it does not make practical sense to use it anymore. For example, if you have a vehicle that meets your needs, is operational, and will not cost more to repair than replace, then why buy a new one? The same can be said for a myriad of other electronics, clothes, furniture, etc. Save your money, buy good quality goods, and then use what you buy until it just cannot be used anymore. Wear it out and make do are great slogans for living within your budget. You do not have to be Ebenezer Scrooge to be thrifty. You just need to remember that everything, including your time, has a monetary value. Sometimes, it makes more sense to do without something than to buy and own it. If the potential thing you want to buy will take away your focus from your business and family, do not buy it. If it will cause you to forget who you are and where you came from, you do not need it.

To wrap this up, let me add that for big purchases it is always good to shop online first, go look at it in the store if you need to. After you have looked at the item, go home and think about it for 24 hours before you buy. Do not get pressured into buying something on the spot, you are smarter than that. Know the price before you go back to make a purchase and then negotiate for a better deal. Where possible, pay for big expenses in cash and insist on a discount. Store managers will often give you a deal on big ticket items if you just ask and negotiate a little. Remember, cash is king and makes it easier to bargain.

Sam Walton, the founder of Wal-Mart, understood these principles well and practiced them. He could have used his money in any way he wanted. Instead, he chose to drive a 7-year-old pickup truck and wore clothes that he sold in his stores. Someone visiting his Bentonville, Arkansas, community, who did not know who he was, would likely have overlooked him. In 1992, at the time of his death, Sam Walton was worth $65 billion. Yet he was driving a red 1985 Ford pickup truck and living in the same house he had been in since 1959.

Learn to Repair What is Worth Repairing: This is a challenging concept because it almost seems to scream in the face of the idea that everything has value including your time. However, there are some guidelines for repairing those things that have lasting value. I am a big believer in buying the best I can afford. I do not generally buy name brand clothing. If I do, it is because I got them on sale or at a thrift store. I shop for the best things I can afford. What I have learned in trying to live a thrifty lifestyle is that sometimes you have to say no. You have to say no, I love this excellent product but the cost of repairing it, or paying someone to repair it, is not worth the time I will spend messing with it.

If you are new in your business, this idea can be particularly challenging as sometimes you have to spend money you do not want to spend. In the early days of one business, doing editing and desktop publishing, I had a printer that I loved. It was given to me, and it worked great most of the time. However, it was prone to jamming losing half of a print job if I printed over a certain number of pages at one time. It was frustrating and slowed me down a bit, but I learned to work with it until I had the money to replace it. I just printed few pages at a time. I had the certified printer repair training from my day job, so I continued to repair whatever needed to be fixed on the printer while I used it. The printer would work for another couple of months and then would go back to messing up again. The problem was not the repair job, but the quality of the printer hardware. I worked with it for as long as was economically viable.

I finally had to stop repairing the printer because I was losing production time messing with it all the time. I finally bought a new printer and all the sudden I was free to focus on my business. All the sudden, I had time to get more done because I did not have to nurse the printer along. Working with the faulty printer made sense up to a point, and then I had to look at my lost productivity. Having more time to focus on my customers and business was far more valuable once I got to a certain point. The economics of repair changed because my business grew. I held on to that printer for as long as I could because I had wanted to save money by not buying a new one. What I discovered was that I was wasting time which also had a dollar value attached to it once I got to a certain size and volume of customers. One of the lessons I had to learn that I am trying to share here is that I had not realized how much time I was spending on the printer until it was gone. I know this is a minor example but that is the whole point. The simple lesson here is if you own something good enough do not get another one just because it is new. However, if that tool is broken and you are wasting time and money to work on it all the time, it may be time to move on and get a replacement. You have better things to spend your time on.

Before we leave this idea and move on to the next, I want to touch on the importance of skills development. We will touch on this more later. However, I cannot stress enough that learning how to repair what is worth repairing, can lead to interesting ways to expand your business opportunities. Little did I know that my skills learning how to repair printers would be so helpful many years down the line. Because I had spent so much time working on printers in my full-time job and in our business, I was able to find some printers that were used and really needed a cleaning. I found them sitting on a pallet outside of an office building that was being renovated. I went inside to ask about them and I was told they were being thrown away and that I could have them if I wanted them. I took all six printers home. I used parts from two of the printers, that were beyond repair, to fix the other four and then turned around and sold the four printers. My skills developed in learning how to repair printers and sell them. This allowed me to put more money back into our business.

One Man's Junk is Another Man's Jacket: Even if you are a millionaire from your business, you are not too good to shop at a thrift store. Macklemore & Ryan Lewis may have been on to something when they were popping tags at their local thrift store. Despite the stigma that some have about thrift stores, the fact remains that there are a lot of really good ways to save money when shopping for the right kind of items. This is especially true with children who can sometimes jump a size seemingly overnight. Some of the items that can be good deals at thrift stores are jeans, jackets, shirts, blazers, sweaters, tops, skirts, dresses, slacks, and books. With a little effort, you can even find days when your local thrift store will give great deals on their already low prices. One of our local thrift stores has a deal that everything with a specific color tag was 50% off for a specific day of the week. If you go with cash in hand, you can stick to your budget and clothe yourself in functional fashion. There are, of course, some things that you should avoid purchasing at thrift stores. Those items include, (in my opinion) used shoes (sometimes there are exceptions), underclothing, swimwear, computers, car seats, mattresses, and pillows.

Fashion is a Foul Mistress: Perhaps your mother told you this as a kid. She may have said it in a different way, but the lesson here is still the same – "focus on function, not fashion." That is not to say you should not wear fashionable clothing. It simply means that following fads and trends is not a great way to save money and get out of debt. Conservative styles never go out of fashion and make a statement that you are to be trusted, are stable, and credible. Isn't that really the message you want to convey about your business? You want people to feel comfortable and confident that the money they are spending with you and your business is in good hands. They want the confidence they will receive delivery of high-quality products and services. How you dress and how you present yourself is often the difference in first impressions and finally solidifying the sale. Fad fashions do not present the image of longevity and stability in business. As a small business owner, when you are in front of your customers, you need to present the best image of stability you can possibly project.

The image of stability is a hard concept to qualify but is worth a quick review. If you are a trained plumber and show up in a business suit to your customer's house, you are not dressed properly. You are overdressed and not functionally attired for fixing the plumbing under the sink. A pair of functional work pants and a matching logoed work shirt are the right image for this type of business. On the other hand, if your business is a consulting company where you are dealing with C-level executives, then a suit is the right functional attire. The rule here is simple; focus on your image and what potential customers will see as a first impression. You do not have to blow your budget to look sharp and present a professional image. If you plan and shop judiciously, you can really make a good first impression.

I think it is important to add a comment about business suits for men and women. If you need to wear a suit for your small business, then save and buy the best you can afford. There is nothing that looks worse that an untailored suit coat or blazer. If you must save up for a good suit, and can only afford one, then focus on getting something that fits you well. Suits do not have to be expensive. If it is tailored correctly, an inexpensive suit can create a solid impression. Take the time to get a proper measuring and get your suit coats and pants tailored. In my opinion, every business owner should own a suit (for women a pants or dress suit) that they have in their closet ready at a moment's notice to make a "big impression." You never know when one of your customers might invite you to a luncheon, get together, or conference at the spur of the moment. They may introduce you to bigger customers that can bring you to a new level of business. In my experience, being ready with the right clothing and a polished pair of shoes has been a powerful tool. I have been able to enter those situations confident in who I was and how I was dressed. I made myself and my business look good. My suits may have been thrift store suits for a lot of years, but when they fit me correctly, it did not matter. I now work to purchase nice, tailored suits but still buy several blazers second-hand. I can tell you that unless I told you, you would never have known.

Cook at Home and Brown Bag Leftovers: A great way to be thrifty is to avoid eating out for lunch with your day job. It is not like your lunches will be free as you still had to pay for the food you prepared. What it really boils down to is that you can eat for a lot less per meal. As an added bonus, you will not be spending gas money to go grab something to eat. By bringing your own lunch, you can save a tremendous amount of money over the course of a year. If your burger, fries, and a drink cost you $10.00 each meal and your lunch from home only costs you $3.00, you are saving $7.00 every day. If you take the average number of workdays a year (250) and multiply that out, you could save $1,750 a year. That is enough for an inexpensive weekend family vacation or an extra house payment to pay down a mortgage quicker.

Saving that amount of money could be all you need to start a part time business on the side. Besides, as a part time small business owner, you should save your restaurant meals for meetings with clients; it is a tax-deductible expense. Of course, if you do not spend the money on lunches, you could also spend it taking your significant other out on some nice "parent's night out" and still be able to afford a babysitter. This means you are more likely to pick better restaurants, go to the theater, or some other fun outing. Not only will brown bagging lunch save you money, but it might also improve your marriage. Money saved can be used for a very nice dinner once a month with your sweetheart. Having a nice dinner with uninterrupted communication with your spouse is a sure way to fall in love all over again.

Bicycling is a Great Way to Save and stay Healthy: As a self-proclaimed bicycling fanatic, I could not miss this chance to tell you that cycling is a great tool in living a thrifty life. Whenever you can, commute by bicycle. It is a great way to stay healthy and save a lot of money. For most of us in the US, living closer to our day jobs and cycling could equal thousands of dollars in savings annually. Once your business is up and running successfully and you transition from part time to full time, you can use your bicycle for quick errands. It saves wear and tear on your car and costs a fraction of a penny to operate per mile. If you desire to run a green business, bicycles can even be part of your marketing focus and product delivery. Even if you are not able to bicycle to commute, using it to help maintain your fitness is worth the effort. Healthy people tend to be more energetic and happier. Energetic and happy people almost always have better sales outcomes in my experience.

Avoid Thrift Myths: I am going to go out a limb here and say something that I will probably catch a bunch of grief for, but I think it needs to be said. First, you cannot save yourself to wealth. It is a full on lie perpetuated by the banking industry that saving alone will allow you to retire in style. There is no way it can. How can saving alone on an income where you are living in debt going to get you to a better lifestyle of comfort after you retire?

The buying value of your dollars keeps going down each year and the average return on mutual funds alone is probably never going to catch up with the rate of inflation. If you want to get ahead, you must find ways to live well below your income level and find a way to make more money. Avoid those people that will tell you about some get rich schemes or that getting rich slowly from savings. Without living below your income level and making more, you will not get ahead. The only exception to this rule, in my opinion is when you have a financial planner and consultant who is actively managing investments for you and who is fully focused on your benefit and outcome. They are out there, but there are few and far between. If you find someone you can work with who will help you to truly have better returns than standard mutual fund investing, then I would change my general opinion.

Some of you who are reading this may think, 'Well, if all I need to do is make more money than a part time job is all I need. Why do I need to start a business?' Let me begin my comments by saying I am a huge Dave Ramsey fan. I think his advice about getting a part time job for most people is a smart move. For those who are not concerned about what they do and who simply want to get out of debt, then a part time job is the perfect option. I agree that using your income in a logical manner to pay down debt is critical for financial freedom. But is it really applying a new way of thinking? Not really. It is just applying what you know to a problem that got you broke to begin with.

Without changing the way they think, most people will start a part time job and then will over time increase their expenditures to match their new income. In my experience, this is because their way of thinking has not changed. They are mentality still just an employee. If you want to change your circumstance, you must change the way you think. Part time jobs are for most people just a way to make more money to spend.

When a person understands that they must change the way they think to get out of debt, they need to do something different. Besides, part time jobs generally pay very little as you are relegated business leftovers. These are jobs that cannot be done in the daytime. If all you are concerned about is debt reduction, then a part time job may be an acceptable last choice but is a poor one at best. For a unique group of people, getting out of debt is only part of what they really need and want. For those that desire more than debt reduction, a part time job alone is not going to meet your needs. These folks realize life is not just about making more money; it is about making a lifestyle change. Starting your own part-time business may not always produce an income as quickly, but when planned correctly, it can produce long and lasting benefits.

Owning your own company requires hard work, it requires learning, and it requires definition. To be successful, you need to define what you want to accomplish and set the goals and milestones you want to achieve. Most small business owners say what makes the difference is that they are in charge and get to call the shots. They, through their own planning, get to determine to a great degree their own level of success. Passion alone will not make you successful in a small business, but defining what you do and making a difference for your customers is the best part of owning your own business. Even if it needs to be part time to begin with.

Practicing thrift is a wise choice for small business owners who want to make the most of their efforts and keep what they earn. Look for ways to cut costs by reducing, recycling, and reusing what you can. People who practice thrifty living often become passionate about it. In fact, you may very well find that your learned passion for thrifting could build a nice small business in and of itself. There are plenty of people looking to save money and stretch the money they already make. They may not have the passion to start a business like you do, but they would make great customers.

In the next section, we are going to expand on the idea of thrifting and providing for your family. We are going to discuss how gardening, food storage, and emergency preparedness are great ways to live thrifty. These tools are part of the plan for ensuring you can continue to build your business even when sales slowdown and emergencies happen.

Section 2: Feed Me and Just in Case: Food Freedom & Preparation

In this section, we will cover the areas of preparation and reserves for sustaining your business when there are down cycles. Every business owner will experience fluctuations in their business efforts and income. The principles of emergency preparedness, gardening, and food reserves (or food insurance) are tools in the freedom matrix that help to smooth out the rough spots so you can concentrate on your business success. The elements discussed in this section are examples of the mindset difference needed to become a sustainable entrepreneur when your business is buffering or in a slowdown.

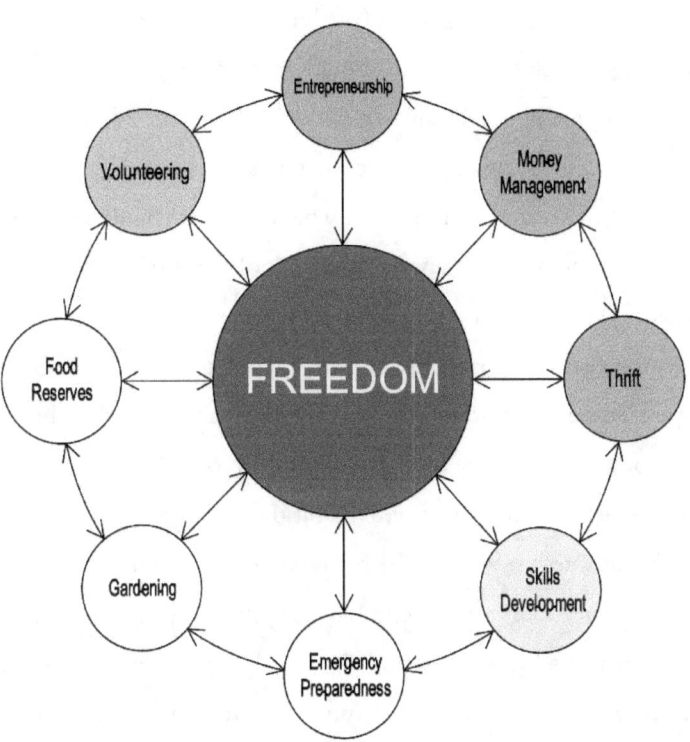

Chapter 4: Gardening

Gardening is a classic skill that should be developed by everyone but especially a small business owner. Gardening stretches dollars and makes sense. It really does not matter what area your small business is in, growing a garden is a great idea. So, what does gardening have to do with a small business? Let us answer that by looking at the life of the small business entrepreneur.

Santiago opened his part time business two years ago while still working a fulltime job. Within 36 months, he was able to replace his day job income. He took the plunge and decided to go full time in his business. Things are going great until he hit the 18-month mark full-time into his business solely, and he runs into a sales slump. It is not because he has been less attentive to his business; it is just a seasonal sales slump or just a low sales period. Santiago's current sales leads will likely produce more sales in the near future, but that may take some time. For many business owners, this is when they panic because they are taking money too early in their business or they have not built up a cash reserve. However, as a wise steward of his earnings, Santiago has been holding a significant percentage of his business earnings. He has been maintaining cash reserves for six months of operating expenses minus paying himself. With the cash reserves on hand, he will be able to keep supporting his customers and build up his potential client base while there is no current cash flow.

Santiago also saved up a nice little personal emergency fund to pay his personal bills and a couple months of mortgage payments for his house. His emergency funds are for bills, but he also needs to feed his family until he can pay himself again from his business. If Santiago had some food set aside (we will talk about food reserves in the next chapter) and a garden, he would hardly miss a beat. He could continue to feed himself and his family while still meeting his financial obligations and growing his business. Santiago is a prime example of what it means to be a sustainable entrepreneur. While not something often considered important to growing your business, we found growing a garden is a great way to supplement your small business income to stretch your dollar a little further. This non-orthodox approach to supporting sustainability for a small business is an amazing tool for keeping spirits high and your health strong.

You do not have to have a large garden plot to grow a lot of food. If planned correctly, a 100 square foot garden (10' X 10') can grow a tremendous amount of produce. I would love to give you exact numbers, but the answer really depends on you and where you live. In my personal experience, our family grew a little over 120 pounds of vegetables in a growing season. Our garden included lettuce, tomatoes, peppers, onions, potatoes, okra, green beans, and various herbs. All these things we were able to eat, and we did not have to spend gas money going to the store to purchase them thus our expenses were also lower. You will likely not make money with your garden. That is not really the point. It is another tool to have and use on your way to financial freedom. It serves as a balancing force in reminding a business owner that businesses, like gardens are a result of reaping what you sow.

You do not have to be a gardening wizard to grow a small garden. You are not likely a business genius either, are you going to let that stop you? Of course not, you go out and learn what you need to know and move on. In fact, learning what and how to grow is also great for teaching your kids about nature and being thrifty. In my experience, food that you raise always tastes better and is nutritionally better for you than what you can purchase in a grocery store. If you will focus on raising nutritionally dense foods, you will give your family the nutrition that most of our modern diets are lacking. In the process, you will also be feeding their minds with the value of hard work. If you can instill in your children the value of hard work and reaping what they sow, you will be preparing them for the future. Think of what that would do for them. It would prepare them to be entrepreneurial in their own thinking. You will be teaching them that hard work sometimes comes with some disappointments and awesome rewards.

Gardening: During the 1930's families found the US Government encouraged families to garden to feed themselves due to the existing economic hardships of the Great Depression. These became known as Great Depression Gardens. During this time, families would plow under the grass in their backyards (grass is not exactly the wisest invention ever nor the best use of personal land, but that is a whole other topic) and grow a garden. These gardens were heavily planted with vegetables which could be eaten fresh or stored for consumption during the winter. The modern casseroles are an example of the kinds of dishes created during depressions and economic downturns. These allowed for the use of many garden ingredients and were generally a much cheaper meal to prepare.

Entrepreneurs are unique in their desire to develop their own independence and self-sustainability. The generally overlooked and forgotten craft of gardening has been removed from our business ownership and self-sustaining equation by convenience. However, grocery store fruits and vegetables that meet strict industrial storage and longevity requirements are not the benefit one may at first consider. These industrial food options come at the price of produce variety, taste, and nutrition. While these industrial farmed produce options are pretty and uniform, they are not as flavorful or tastefully satisfying as locally grown (or self-grown) produce. I would also argue they are not as nutritionally valuable as well, but I will leave that for others to debate. What I can say is that there are fruit and vegetable varieties, that are easy to grow, that will never be on grocery shelves and are just amazing.

For anyone that needs to experience this for themselves go to a local farm co-op or farmers market where produce is locally grown and then sold by the farmer. Compare a locally grown and freshly harvested apple, tomato, or peach and you will never want another supermarket one again. Once you consider the power of a garden in allowing you to maintain your entrepreneurial sustainability, you will take and make the time to garden as part of your business and personal life planning. It will be a powerful tool of education and sustaining you and your family.

Planting Fruit Trees: If you own your own home, consider planting fruit trees in your yard. It is a great way to improve the value of your property and feed yourself in the process. When you take this in conjunction with a garden, you have even more food options. I know of one business owner who needed new equipment for his lawn care business but did not have the money he needed to make a purchase and stay out of debt. He was able to trade the crops from his peach and plum trees for a new lawn tractor. Your fruit trees and garden, while not being a huge money maker, may mean the difference in paying employees or eating. Always pay your employees first, but I really like the idea of doing both. Preparation for anything and knowing you can always rely on your garden if you need to, is like having your own personal food insurance policy. A policy where the only deductible is the effort you put into it.

Before you say, 'Hey, I do not have room to grow a big tree in my yard,' consider that many garden centers sell dwarf fruit trees that take less room than a traditional fruit tree while still producing a great fruit. As you think about what to plant in your yard, take the time to do your homework about what you want and what will grow where you live. As much as I love the big hardware store retailers (and I do love to walk the aisles), just remember they are not gardening experts and many of the trees and garden items supplied by them each spring may not grow where you live. I recommend working with a local nursery and garden center that has experts on what will grow in your local area. As you work with them or with a state university agricultural extension you will get a better idea what will grow and produce well in your area.

As you begin to select trees for your yard, make sure to meet all your local zoning requirements and select appropriate trees for your area accordingly. You will also probably want to look up the USDA plant hardiness zone for your area. Once you know what plants and varieties grow best in your area you can then look at what your local discount store or hardware store for plants that will produce fruit in your area. While I recommend this to save money, I also see the need to support small local businesses and often split my purchases between both. I know if I support the local nursery, they are going to be around year after year as I need to learn more or add more food producing plants in my yard. At the end of the day, the whole point is to plant trees and produce fruit according to your growing zone, conditions, and space. You will avoid silly and sometimes expensive mistakes like planting a lemon tree in your back yard in Idaho. (However, you might be able to grow a miniature Meyer Lemon tree in a pot inside your house if you are willing to learn about growing and nurturing the tree.)

We have practiced this principle in our own yard and home so we can produce as much of our own food as possible. We have an apple tree, cherry trees, plum trees, raspberry bushes, Gooseberry bushes, and a strawberry patch. Each year we plant tomatoes, peppers, and herbs in pots on our backyard deck. We have two beehives in our backyard to pollinate our garden and trees as well as produce a limited amount of honey each year. These are supplemented with fig bushes and lemon, lime, and orange trees in our home which are under grow lights in the house during the winter (they go outside in the warm summer months). I am always continuing to develop and learn new growing skills for different plants. For example, I am currently learning how to grow lettuce in a homemade hydroponics system I created out of plastic storage totes. If I am successful, we will be able to have fresh lettuce for salads all year long. I am currently growing six different kinds of lettuce in my system.

If You Cannot Garden, at Least Join a Co-op: Reducing the cost of your grocery bill and keeping yourself within your budget are critical to your success. For some people, planting a garden or fruit trees is simply not an option. If you are living in an apartment or rental house, it may be a space or permission problem. For others, their health will simply not allow them to grow and maintain a garden. If this is the case for you, consider joining a farm co-op. There are organizations like Bountiful Baskets Food Co-op and other local co-ops where individuals can contribute towards the purchasing of produce in season. It is a great way to stay within your budget and improve the nutritional value of the food your family eats. If something like Bountiful Baskets is not available in your area, visit your local farmer's market and inquire about co-ops there.

As a last option, if you cannot find a local co-op, consider buying in-season produce in bulk with your friends and family from your local grocery store. It may not give you better produce, but it will reduce your food bill overall. Many grocery chains will offer discounts if you buy enough product in bulk. If your grocery store will not deal with you, then shop somewhere else. The end result should be to reduce your food costs so do not buy these purchases on credit. Save your money and buy these purchases with cash you saved up and planned to use for food. By taking these steps, you are far more likely to eat healthier. As you eat healthier you can maintain and use your energy for growing your business.

Small Scale Meat Production: If you are up to adding more than a garden, you can raise your own animals for food production. Some great animals that fit into most areas are rabbits, chickens, or even quail. If you are adventurous and really want to try something cool, consider a greenhouse aquaponics system. Aquaponics is the combination of raising vegetables and fish in a symbiotic relationship. If the idea of dispatching animals is more than you can handle, find a local butcher or meat market, and try to buy whole and half animal meat package deals to save money.

Over the course of our lives my wife and I have been involved in raising lots of animals for food and food production. This has included raising dairy and beef cattle, sheep, goats, pigs, chickens, rabbits, and quail. If you have the capacity and place to raise meat for personal family consumption, there is a lot of value added and the benefit of knowing what your livestock consumed and that it was raised and harvested in an ethical and humane way. Of course, these things are beyond the scope of this book but are ideas for reducing the cost of feeding your family and are great food insurance options for your building your business.

Chapter 5: Food Reserves and Preservation

I know this may come as a shock, but sometimes life is hard. Sometimes individuals and small businesses hit roadblocks, have slowdowns, or must rethink what they do altogether. The tragedy is that many talented and successful entrepreneurs are knocked off their feet by these events and end up out of business. It happened to me twice because I was unprepared and unable to ride out the storm. I like to think I am a fairly smart guy, but when my main customer decided they did not need my services anymore, I was left with a 50% cut in my monthly earnings. In another business, my supply chain dried up and my raw material costs jumped up 30% virtually overnight. Of course, my customers were not willing to pay the passed-on increases. It was the beginning of the end because I had no reserves and could not retool and rethink my business with needed reserves and time. Plain and simple I could not feed my family and I had to give up my dream and get a job working for someone else. I had to learn the hard way the lessons I am now sharing with you in this book. I had to learn to manage my money better, to be thrifty (painfully by default and not by choice), and that building a food reserve is a powerful tool for entrepreneurs. I learned having a food reserve was a cheap insurance policy for a small business and the family I was supporting. In this chapter, I am going to share some reasons to store food, and then, briefly touch on methods for building up a food reserve so you can survive a business slowdown or business retooling period. I will share with you how this can help you hold on and turnaround toward greater success.

Having a Food Reserve (Food Insurance) is Great Freedom Insurance: Business downturns and life's little emergencies are not rare. Even the best plans cannot account for all the risks associated with starting your own business. In the most successful small businesses, there are always going to be hiccups. These issues can slow down your growth or put a stop to your earning potential entirely if you are not prepared. Without fail, these not-so-wonderful, unexpected tragedies hit when we are least prepared. For me, some of those things were a massive monthly mortgage hike after an updated tax assessment, a home air conditioner replacement in Texas in August, being unable to work for two weeks (because of a flu, bronchitis, and Asthma triple punch), and a myriad of other things. Life is unpredictable and you simply never know what is going to happen. These were not the end of the world catastrophes. These were just common things that hit and hurt us along the way. For those working a small business as a supplemental income, these may not be as impactful. However, as your business matures and grows and becomes a fulltime journey, these events can be the difference between a negative or a positive growth month. What we found in our experience was that having a food reserve, or what I like to call food insurance, at our home allowed us to feed ourselves while we nursed our business and ourselves back to health. Of all the insurance policies you can have, for yourself and your business, food insurance is one of the cheapest and most practical. If you can eat, then you can remain calm, think, and work through the issues. To make a food reserve, or food insurance work, you are going to need to apply some simple rules.

Do Not Get Further in Debt for a Food Reserve: The number one rule you should never break when it comes to food reserves is do not get fancy and get into debt for your food. There are plenty of folks out there that would be willing to sell you a year's worth of food for a truckload of money or on credit. Do not do it! There is no reason whatsoever to spend thousands of dollars on a package deal for food you will not eat. Focus on storing what you can and will eat at a price you can afford. Make sure it is within your budget for whatever you add to your food reserves. Once you are out of debt and you have the ability and desire to buy a package deal then go ahead and buy it. Heck, if you want to go ahead and buy a 3-month supply of freeze-dried fruit. To begin with, focus on the basics that will sustain you and keep you moving forward.

There is no reason you should end up on an episode of *Doomsday Preppers* with what you are storing. This is not that kind of overzealousness. I understand that some people are preparing for the magnetic poles to shift or for the zombie apocalypse. Those things are not on my risk list for my business or my family and probably should not be on yours. Be practical and focus on what you like to eat, what will keep you alive, and keep your hunger under control. This will allow you to make your business successful without having to think about your stomach. (If your small business is focused on preparing people for the Zombie uprising forget everything I just said; maybe you know something I don't.)

Store What You Eat and Eat What You Store: The most important rules of building a food reserve comes down to a few things. First, store only what you will eat for the amount of time you estimate your potential crises will be. The idea is to feed yourself and your family, so you can focus on retooling your business. Second, food reserves should be rotated with your regular groceries and be part of what you eat regularly. This becomes easier as you include vegetables from your garden and fruit from your trees as it will allow you to use the freshest produce right from your back yard. If you mix what you store with what you grow and rotate your food reserve, you will avoid having unusable expired items.

Finally, sometimes sharing from your food reserves is a much better way to help extended family and friends in need. We have found sharing produce from our garden and a couple of boxes of food from our food reserves with friends (or adult children) in need is often the best way to extend a helping hand. When you have built your business up to where you are debt free, you can become Aunt and Uncle Moneybanks until then food is a great way to help others in need. We will discuss helping others out in Chapters 7 and 9. Keep in mind, sometimes people just need something to eat to get them through a rough patch. Often, they will accept food when they will not accept money.

Learn How to Preserve Your Own Food: Nothing is more rewarding than pulling jars from your food reserves that you grew and preserved yourself. If I can be a bit dramatic here, it is just tragic that there is a whole generation of young people who have never experienced the joy of homemade canned pickles, jams, or jellies. Even more lamentable is when they have never enjoyed home-canned peaches, apricots, or applesauce. I am not hinting that it makes your life incomplete by not trying those things. I am just saying that not experiencing the joy of eating these things is just plain sad.

What a real tragedy it would be to grow food in your garden and on your fruit trees and let it go to waste because you cannot eat it all at once. This is especially true when you consider that people have been canning at home since the 1860's. With the advent of super and mega market grocery chains people stopped growing their own gardens and food at home. The result is that we eat far more processed food and have moved farther away from home-based food production. The disaster of it all is that those processed foods are really, in the end, far more expensive nutritionally speaking. However, that is a topic for another book. The point is that canning what you grow makes a lot of sense. Once you have invested in the equipment then the canning process is easy to learn and very economical. As an added benefit, getting your kids involved in gardening and then food preservation is a fantastic way to teach them where food comes from and the work that is involved in feeding a family. Kid's that learn the value of work early, learn to earn and hold on to what they make. Teaching kids the value of work is a lesson that pays off in lifelong dividends.

One of the best methods for increasing what you have in your food reserves is to grow or buy in-season fruits and vegetables and then can them. With a little experience you can buy meat in bulk and try canning meats, stews, and chili with amazing results. As with all canning and food preservation, use reputable and current resources and follow the directions. Do not try to wing it. You will just create a problem for your family's health and waste food and money. Canning food is labor intensive at times, but it is sweat equity food insurance for your family and your business. It is well worth the effort!

I Cannot Can Food: I shared with one woman the principle of canning as a freedom building tool and she looked at me and said, "I can't do that, I don't even know how to cook. Shoot, I can burn water." After laughing and telling her that it was not as hard as she thought, I told her about another method that she could probably handle. I told her she could use the one extra can method to build up her food reserves. The one extra can method is very simple. When you shop for groceries, pick up one extra can of everything you buy. Of course, you still need to stay within your budget, so it may not be a can every trip. By adding an extra can for each of the items she buys, she would be building up a nice little reserve in no time at all. Now, there are, of course, some draw backs to this method. First, not everything comes in a can that we eat. Second, some things in a can are, well, nasty and not worth storing. Of course, some of that is personal choice. I personally think canned peas should be illegal. The answer to this is to form a plan and store only what you can logically rotate and will eat within its acceptable shelf life. Some boxed goods like pasta and rice can last for a long time if stored in an airtight container. The one extra can method is a good alternative but may require some creativity to get a proper and nutritional food mix.

Where Do I Store My Food Reserves?: I have to be honest here, this is that point where I have to look back at you with a puzzled look. The answer is that it all depends on you and your priorities. Personally, we store food in places all over the house. We store food in the pantry, under beds, bedroom closets, and shelving setup just for food. Some of you may be saying, wait! I do not have room in my closets for more stuff. Why not? Got too much junk in your closets? Maybe it is time to get rid of some of the extra things out of your closet. Who knows you might be storing stuff you have not used in years that could be seed money for starting your business or launching another product. If you have things you have not used in years, you probably do not need them anyway. Make a clean start, sell some things you do not need, and clear some space. You could use the money to jumpstart your food insurance.

What you store and how you store your food reserves is a personal choice. Just remember, that it is an insurance policy you take out on yourself for yourself. If you are wise in your management of your resources, you will quickly find it will bring a lot of peace of mind when problems occur. The next part of the process of building your food reserves is performing an emergency preparedness review. We will talk about this in greater detail in the next chapter.

Chapter 6: Emergency Preparedness

Regardless of how well we try to avoid them sometimes, big emergencies happen. Thank goodness they do not happen all the time, but they do happen. When they do, they can have a massive impact on small business entrepreneurs. Planning for those emergencies, beyond building and maintaining your food reserves, is important for the continuity of your business and lifestyle. In my personal experience, being able to get back to work after an emergency is the greatest kind of therapy. In this chapter, we will discuss things you can do to prepare for and mitigate the risks associated with emergencies. One of the first things we need to do is assess what kind of realistic emergencies are more likely to happen. Some emergencies can be geographically based such as tornados, earthquakes, etc. Others can be seasonal events like ice storms, blizzards, and other weather events. To clarify, these are not typical events where the next morning everyone goes about their lives and comments on their disturbed sleep. These are the kind of emergencies that cause the traffic of commerce to stop for a week at a time. These kinds of events, we want to plan for, are the kind of events that keep us from serving our customers and making sales.

Avoiding Data Emergencies

Keep Your Business Data Secure: Before we discuss the emergencies that are from the outside, we need to make sure we are covering any potential inside issues. Your business and pretty much every other business relies on information. Whether you have a prize cookie recipe or are keeping financial records secure, you must think in terms of acceptable loss. The key is come up with a plan that will help you to avoid data losses in any way. Depending on the size of your business having all your sales and customer records on a single computer is not all that uncommon. It is really dumb, but it is not uncommon. What happens if your hard drive crashes and you lose that critical data? There is no reason you should put yourself in that kind of position. There are countless inexpensive ways to backup and store your data to keep it secure.

If you are just starting out, consider investing in at least an external hard disk drive or a thumb drive as a daily backup. Keep the back up in a different place than the computer. It is a good idea to store the external storage device in a fireproof box. Fireproof boxes range from about $45.00 and up and are an important item for storing vital business paperwork. Keep your important legal documents and data backup in a fireproof box and keep the box safe. Make sure you backup on a daily, or at least, a regular basis. If you are prone to forget to perform backups, make sure to set yourself a calendar item. As a reminder, fireproof boxes are really a very simple and less than perfect solution. Afterall, "fireproof" is really a generous definition of what these boxes do. They do provide some theft and fire protection, but it is minimal given the portability and fire rating of the boxes currently available. Just consider that a small home safe or fire box may give you about an hour as long as the fire stays under 1,700 degree Fahrenheit (about 926 degrees Celsius). For most small business owners with critical customer data, this is a cheap but less than perfect data storage and backup solution.

Given the number of online cloud storage options and the ability to encrypt data online cloud storage may be a much better option for most small businesses. Cloud based data storage and backups are far more common than many people think. They are used by nearly every internet user or smart phone owner who stores some data "online". If you have paid for iCloud services with your iPhone, you have used cloud storage. Other services for Android phones include Box, Dropbox, and Sync.com to name a few. These services will generally charge you an annual or monthly fee for a set amount of storage but may have entry level options with limited storage for free. As I tell business owners all the time, you pay for what you get. When you get it for free, you are guaranteed nothing. Keep in mind, these services are generally inexpensive if you consider the cost of lost data. Cloud storage and backups often come with an additional feature which is a real plus for small business owners. They allow you to access data and files from anywhere you can connect to the internet. If you use an internet connected tablet, laptop, or smartphone, then you can access data while you are speaking with your customers in their place of business. Not all online storage services are fully secure, so make sure whatever you choose has built in login two-factor authentication security controls and encryption. In my businesses and for my customers, I recommend a few different options. If you are an Apple product enthusiast, then I recommend using iCloud as it works seamlessly on your Mac, iPad, and iPhone. If you are a PC and Android user, then I recommend using Dropbox. These are my own personal choices and do not reflect an endorsement, just my personal experience. (As a sideline note iCloud and Dropbox can be used for both PCs and Apple computers.)

Keep in mind, the point of your backups is to ensure you can get your business up and selling products and services as soon as possible, if an emergency occurs. You need to manage your backup strategy proactively and answer any issues before they become problems. Make sure to test restoring files from your backup to make sure there are no problems. Do not let circumstances dictate how and if you can run your business. If you focus on realistic risks, not dreamed up scenarios, you will be able to meet them successfully and get past them quickly.

Protect Payment Card and Personal Customer Information: As companies like Target, Michaels, and T.J.Maxx can tell you, suffering a data breach is both painful and embarrassing. However, big box retailers are not the only companies that can suffer devastating data breaches. Companies of all sizes and shapes are just as, if not more, likely to experience a data breach. Your small business may not process a massive number of credit card or debit card transactions. However, a data breach and loss of customer data or credit card data can shut your business down. Complying with the Payment Card Industry Data Security Standard (PCI) is your responsibility. Every business owner large or small who accepts payment cards for their business needs to know what PCI is. We cannot cover all the requirements for PCI compliance here, but suffice it to say you are on the hook for your customer's private data and credit card information. If you decide to accept credit or debit cards, you will need to work closely with your credit card processing company to make sure your business practices will keep information secure and safe. I did my doctoral dissertation on this topic, and I can assure you it is important for every business to be compliant even if you think you're not at risk, you are. There really is no excuse for not protecting yourself and your customer's data. Your business is built on trust. Do not blow it when it comes to something as important as one of the methods of getting paid. If you are not careful and secure with customer and credit card data, your business may not survive. It is an emergency you can avoid so make sure you do.

Physical & Mental Emergency Preparation

Start with a First Aid Kit: One of the first purchases in your emergency preparedness preparations for your small business should be a first aid kit. In fact, it probably is one of the first things you should get after your business license. It does not have to be a big first aid kit, it just needs to be a functional first aid kit. For the first few months of your business, you need to put it in a prominent place where you will see it every day. I recommend this for a couple of reasons. The first one is for your physical safety. As you move things around and setup for business, you might get a few cuts and scratches. The second reason is that the first aid kit will serve as a reminder. It will remind you that as you start to tell people what you are doing you are going to get some mental cuts and scratches, as well.

No matter how many entrepreneurs I speak to their stories are very similar. They tell friends, family, and coworkers what they are doing part time and the cutting remarks begin. Let the first aid kit serve as a reminder that you are trying something new for yourself, and you may get a scratch along the way. If you are tough enough, you will make it. Just think back to when you were a kid and your mother put a Band-Aid on a cut and you went back out to play. The Band-Aid became your badge of honor. This is no different except now you administer the Band-Aids. The scrapes may come but you have your first aid kit, your dreams, and no one is going to stop you from doing the work to be a success. Overcoming these early emergencies may be the most character-building moments of your life.

Take Time for a Fire Drill: Yes, that is right, take time to practice a fire drill. You need to know how to get out of your office in case of an actual fire. Know where your exits are and how a potential fire will affect your ability to serve your customers. If you do not have a fire plan and a fire should occur, you will panic and not know what to do. Your fire drill should include how you are protecting your data which we spoke about earlier.

There is another kind of fire that can consume business owners. When you have planned well and your business takes off, you must be willing and able to recognize that you have set fire to an idea. You need to remember to have an exit strategy for your mind, body, and spirit. You need to know how to step away from your business long enough to appreciate your success and recognize your failures. Far too many entrepreneurs get so excited with their success and so wrapped up in what to do next and how to fight the next fire that they miss a massively important key to having a life work balance. More than that, constant worrying and never disengaging leads to real life fires that can sometimes destroy friendships, marriages, relationships with others (family, vendors, suppliers, etc.). Running a personal fire drill where you step away from your business and go out to the parking lot "until the alarm stops sounding" may be the most productive thing you can do for your business occasionally. Sometimes seeing your business from the outside instead of always looking at things only from the inside can help you reassess what is important and what you need to do to adjust, modify, or improve processes or procedures. Fire drills help business owners understand the physical and mental fire dangers before they can become real fires that cannot be extinguished.

Owning your own business is work but it is also massively fun. If you take time to step back and look at your business objectively, you will be able to see where you have hot spots and dead branches that could be your next fire. With insight provided by stepping back and a taking a critical view, you will be able to head off these potential fires. The result is you will be able to prevent things from becoming a flame that you have to fight later. Fire drills both actual and figurative are designed to help you think in terms of safety. If you know why you practice your fire drills, you can take the preventive steps needed to avoid a four-alarm fire.

Section 3: Giving and Getting: The Core of Heart Freedom

In Section 1, we covered how you can define your future and make more money through starting a small business. We also covered the principles for managing money and then discussed the ideas of applying thrift to save more of your earned money. In Section 2, we focused on the mindset, principals, and lifestyle tools to prepare your businesses for potential slowdowns. These included feeding yourself while you readjust your business and being prepared for practical life emergencies. In this section, we will discuss ways that you can develop the skills needed to start a business, improve your life, and improve the lives of your fellow beings through volunteering and personal skills development. This section focuses on showing your heart and being actively involved in your community for more than just earning more money.

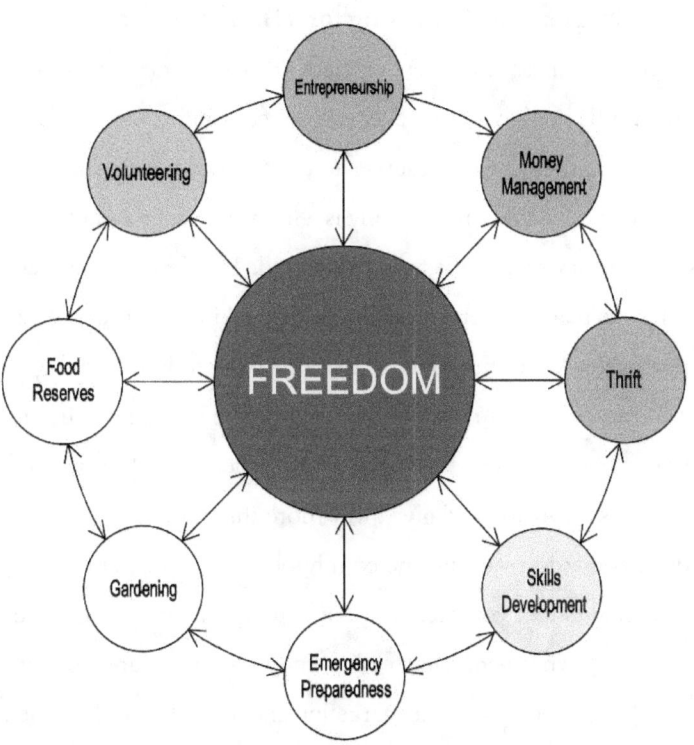

Chapter 7: Volunteering for a Balanced Life

As a small business entrepreneur there are a lot of demands on your time. In this book, we have even suggested using some of your time to build a garden, a food reserve, and to prepare for the most likely emergencies. While this certainly is a lot to consider and plan for, there is a deficiency that needs to be addressed. The deficiency is that these things are really centered on self-based thinking and focus. The problem with this kind of thinking is that it is focused in the wrong direction. Your focus as an entrepreneur should be primarily outbound. Regardless of their respective industry, entrepreneurs need to step out of their business regularly and give away more than what they get. This can be done by getting out into the community and volunteering.

Entrepreneurs that volunteer develop a unique ability to improve their community. They generally need to know the community better so they can be successful in their marketing and sales. Ironically, when small business leaders get involved in the community, they often improve their business in the process. This may sound counterintuitive but in the cosmic order of things, it is vital to your growth as a sustainable entrepreneur. We will discuss this more in Chapter 9. If I can borrow a phrase from James Altucher, you *Choose Yourself*. But you choose yourself to serve others, so you can become successful and those you serve will have enriched lives. You do not have to be someone else. Just volunteer the best *you* possible and share what you can to improve others' lives. Giving to get is a universal law with massive returns on investment.

Successful Businesses Focus on Service First: Whether your business sells a product or provides a service, the secret to success is in the relationships you build and maintain. Those relationships with customers, potential customers, and non-customers alike build your brand. The key to understanding this concept is to realize that everyone you meet has the potential to be a customer or to influence a potential customer. Volunteering in the community is a wonderful way for entrepreneurs to develop relationships. While the focus of your business is to make a profit, you cannot focus on that alone. Focus on how you build relationships first, and you will be able to sell. Volunteering is a great way to build relationships without the pressure to make a sale. Besides, the best business ideas come when businesses are focused on serving others first. Of course, you need to turn a profit if you want to stay in business but not every product or service has to be a money maker. Some products can be provided to those in your community who would benefit from your expertise but cannot afford the gold package. A great book to read, explore, and understand this idea better is *Give and Take* by Adam Grant. He found that companies that give in the community create powerful networks that foster loyalty between companies and customers.

Giving Keeps Your Focus on Real Needs: One of the unique benefits of volunteering is that it provides you with a different focus; something that would be unavailable otherwise. Small business entrepreneurs often get caught in the *busy trap*. This trap is where they are so focused on providing their service and product that they wear blinders. They fail to see how they could expand their offerings to a larger segment of the population.

Let us try a little exercise to illustrate this point. Your business has a total of 1,000 customers and from each of those customers you make a $50 net profit. Most people would agree that the $50,000 earned in a small business is a respectable return for starting a business. For many people, this would be enough for them to quit their full-time job and focus solely on their small business. However, what if you could increase the number of potential customers by having two different products or services? What if some of your services were less expensive to meet the needs of a different client base? This might be the people in the community who you serve as a volunteer. If your business maintained the same 1,000 sales at a $50 net profit, and then added another 1,000 at $35 net profit. Instead of just the $50,000 annually you would be at $85,000 with 2,000 annual customers. Now, which would you rather have? Ironically, there are still entrepreneurs who will stick with the $50K in earnings because they feel like they need to charge $50. They fail to realize the power of volume. They fail to realize their business has to be about people first. They do not understand that diversification of customers and products is a great way to avoid potential sales downturns and is just smart business.

Successful sustainable entrepreneurs who put their priorities in order come to realize sales are a relationship and numbers game. They realize that the more relationships they build the more they will find potential customers. The business owner who must get $50 dollars for every transaction may find there is a shortage of customers able to pay. If an entrepreneur will build a menu of product offerings at $35, $50, and $100, they are likely to have more sales and make more money. Many businesses find that building a tiered system of different product offerings will result in earning much more than with a set price on a single product. This can be the difference between $50,000 or $100,000 or more. In my experience, I have found that when tiered product offerings are made available to customers, they often chose the most expensive option even when cheaper options exist. The point here is that they are given choices and options and nearly everyone likes to have options.

Corporate Citizenship and Sustainability: We have all heard the saying that no man is an island. Well, no business exists in a bubble away from the community where it operates. A business is legally an entity and an organic structure. Just as individuals grow, mature, and progress so do businesses. As living entities, they become citizens of their respective community. As the head of your small business entity, you have a social responsibility to create a business that is beneficial to not only yourself but your community, as well. As we have discussed, volunteering is one of the great ways that you can participate and add benefit to the community. Another way that you can be involved is to run your business in a way that is socially and environmentally conscience. As you practice the elements of sustainable entrepreneurship, you will find it will also have a positive environmental impact. This not the kind of save the world kind of environment. This is the beautify your neighborhood and be a shining example of stable business in your community kind of environmentalism. Gardens may attract bees and butterflies, but stable commerce stabilizes communities and ensures their ability to survive and thrive. Take the time to assess regularly that your business and personal practices reflect your belief that you truly are a vital part of the community in which you live and work.

Mentoring and Charity: Of all the ways you can have a lasting positive impact in your community, mentoring is one with the greatest human dividends. As entrepreneurs, we are always learning, and we can never know everything. However, we learn a lot in the process of our own improvement and there is a lot we can offer to others. There is always someone who does not know what you know and would be grateful for a guiding hand. They may be younger, they may be older, but they can benefit from what you know.

Mentoring does not have to be in person and does not have to take a lot of time. However, it can make a huge difference in the lives of the mentor, the mentee, and the community at large. Think of what a group of mentored business owners could do to improve a dying local old town district. Instead of letting our small communities die, we should be investing in human capital to stop the course of decay and demise. Mentoring in big cities and small communities can pump capital, opportunity, and life into inner cities and rural communities alike. Mentoring can be done by way of phone calls, emails, or cheap lunches. Those that are being mentored often buy lunch or dinner just so they can learn from someone who already knows and is where they want to be. They want to know what you know because as a sustainable entrepreneur you are an inspiration. Mentoring does not have to cost any money, but it almost always provides you with a rewarding return on investment. Give more than you get, and you will illustrate that you and your business are important to the success of every citizen in your community.

Volunteer and Keep Humble: One of the problems with successful business entrepreneurs is we tend to get too big for our britches. We tend to think that we are so important and so busy that we do not have time for others. This is dangerous thinking and is always counterproductive to personal and business progression and long-term success. Your business becomes, is, and will remain successful because of the relationships you build. If entrepreneurs forget their roots, they invariably alienate their customers. What you believe about yourself will shine through in your personality. Customers and potential customers expect you to be successful and enjoy the fruits of your labor. They just do not need you to rub their noses in it.

The second, and far more damaging effect of losing your humility, is the effect that haughty entrepreneurs have on their children and grandchildren. Unfortunately, the saying *rags to riches to rags in three generations* is all too common. But it does not have to be. If entrepreneurs teach their children and grandchildren the value of hard and smart work with some charity thrown in, they can head off these potential family tragedies. Humility is not the responsibility and lot of the poor. It is one of the most powerful tools for using and maintaining wealth. Humble people show gratitude, and gratitude is the only way we can get the wealth we desire without losing ourselves in the process.

Find an Organization with Your Values and Volunteer: There are a lot of nonprofit organizations that survive only by the generosity and volunteering of individuals who share their time and talents. Find a nonprofit organization or church that shares your values and beliefs and get your family to join you in volunteering within that organization. Find a way to spend regular scheduled time making someone else's life better, and you will find your life will be richly rewarded with things that money cannot buy. Organizations that focus on protecting, teaching, and improving the lives of children are always sure bets. If you are personally involved in these organizations, you can always make sure your money and your time are well spent in the most productive manner. Don't be afraid to ask how your money is spent, and do not be afraid to use your hard-earned organizational skills to make your volunteer organization better and more effective.

Chapter 8: Skills Development (The Linchpin Stepping Stone)

Entrepreneurs are generally among the most talented and self-motivated people in the world. They need to be as the very nature of entrepreneurship requires that they rely on themselves more than anyone else. The discussion of what it takes to be a successful entrepreneur often focuses on birth, culture, or training. In other words, are the skills required to be a successful entrepreneur found at birth, are they culturally programmed, or are they things that can be learned? There are, indeed, a few special individuals who seem to instinctively have been born with entrepreneurship in their veins. Then, there are those individuals who by way of culture seem to gravitate towards business ownership and industry. Finally, there is that group of people who seem to defy the masses that pick up the lessons of life and ultimately find themselves in positions of business ownership and entrepreneurship. But is this a perception of reality or reality itself? With a little exploration, it is easy to see that each of these arguments has validity but cannot tell the story of every entrepreneur.

The real challenge in arguing about what makes a successful entrepreneur is that we often do not measure using the correct ruler. If we are using a measurement that is faulty then it will, no matter how many times we hold something up against it, result in the wrong assessment. In this book, we have discussed a lot of different tools to help the sustainability of the small business entrepreneur. We have discussed aspects of money and resource management. We have discussed using thrift, gardening, food reserves, emergency preparation, and volunteering as components of sustainability. If you take a moment to measure it, you quickly come to realize that we did not even discuss the origin of entrepreneurship. The fact is that it does not really matter where it originated. Everyone who has the desire can become what they want to be with enough determination and application of the proper tools. Some people are instinctively entrepreneurial even if their parents are not. Other people receive cultural programming that leads them to an industry where they are self-employed but that does not make them entrepreneurial per se. Then, there are those who know what they do not know and are willing to learn and work to achieve success despite missing knowledge. Those individuals who desire and have the ambition to change their circumstances are the most dominate and successful kind of entrepreneur. If you see yourself in the last definition, you are not alone. You realize that you may not have been bred or programmed for entrepreneurship. However, you are willing to learn what you do not know and are willing to work harder than others to achieve your dream. You realize you are in charge of your own destiny and your own programming. You will do what it takes to develop the skills to become a successful entrepreneur.

Find Your Talents and Develop Marketable Skills: In the harsh reality of life, it is not the most talented that always rise to the top. There are plenty of people who by their IQ are considered a genius but lack ambition and thus are socially and financially unsuccessful. We are not discussing those with mental illness in this definition, of course. We are talking about capable and able-bodied individuals who are gifted by their Creator but are lazy by choice. For most of us, academic and professional success comes at a price. That price is determination and hard work. When we have the determination to discover our hidden talents and to develop marketable skills, we are leveling the playing field in our favor. We do not have to be born the offspring of an entrepreneurial genius. We can become a genius of action in our own right. When we make the decision to apply ourselves to learn what we need to know, practice what we need to do, and learn from our mistakes, we empower ourselves. You may not be the next Albert Einstein, but you can be a genius in making your business a success.

A Mile Wide and a Mile Deep: There is nothing more tragic then when you meet someone who is shallow and uninteresting. My father, who always has great lessons for me, taught me there are a lot of people in the world who work at the same job and do the same thing for ten years are an inch wide and an inch deep. These people can tell you what is on television and all the gossip available but cannot carry on a deep conversation. They live their lives an inch deep and an inch wide. What a tragedy and a waste of this adventure called life. Entrepreneurs cannot afford to be this kind of person.

As an entrepreneur who is building relationships with customers, you need to keep learning and keep developing new skills. Your goal is to be at least a mile wide and a mile deep. You do not have to be an expert at every topic, but you do need to be able to strike up a conversation with everyone you meet. As we discussed in Chapter 7, everyone you meet is a customer, potential customer, or can influence potential customers. If we keep this in mind, we begin to understand we need to be able to converse with everyone. This kind of communication is not idle chit-chat. We need to be able to discuss the important events of the day, life, and a myriad of other topics with our customers. Our conversations need to focus on developing long-term relationships. Customers who feel that they are appreciated and known are going to be more loyal. Creating customer loyalty is the best thing you can do for your business and your customers. These customers will tell their friends about you and will generally spend more money with those companies with whom they are loyal.

As a word of caution, there are a few topics you should never bring up in your conversations with your customers. Some of you instinctively are saying; politics, religion, family, and anything controversial. Actually, with your long term and loyal customers, all of these may be acceptable conversations when deep relationships are developed. You will not know unless you get to know your customers. In my experience talking with customers about sports teams, family, and even local events can be interesting ways to build relationships. You must "read" your customer to really know which topics are okay. As a rule, there are very few people who do not want to tell you about how great their kids are, and every grandparent wants to tell you about their awesome grandkids.

There is only one topic in my experience you should avoid talking about with your customers; do not talk about your competition. If in a discussion with your customers, a comment about your competition comes up kindly change the topic. Change the topic to cover what your business does and can do for your customer. Focus on your relationship with your customer, their needs, and what you can do for them. Just do not talk about your competition. You never need to degrade someone else to elevate yourself or your business. Trust me on this one, I had to learn this the hard way. Negative conversations about your competition leads to negative outcomes and is not part of relationship building, period.

Learn to Sell and Negotiate: Many people will never start an entrepreneurial endeavor for one reason. They think selling is difficult, and they cannot see themselves successfully selling anything. The problem is that they have a misconception of sales. Perhaps this comes from too many product pushers and not enough genuine sales *people*. There are a lot of people that are in the sales game, and they focus on number of sales alone. They push products and convince consumers to buy something they often do not need. However, a real sales professional does not push products they sell themselves and their products as part of a relationship. They are people focused sales people. Your job as a sustainable entrepreneur is to become a relationship builder. As you develop the skills to be a mile deep and a mile wide, you can work on the relationships that engender confidence. When your customers are confident, they will gladly and willingly give you money. If it is a hard sell, then you are doing it wrong. You do not need to force anyone to buy a product. Just take the time to get to know their needs, and if your product is a fit for their needs, you will be able to share it with them (i.e. sell them).

Building a relationship does not mean you will not have to negotiate a deal for what you sell. The art of negotiation is the ability to come to an arrangement that is mutually agreeable and beneficial. Do not be afraid to make a deal when it builds relationships. You do not have to give your products away, but you may want to bend a little now and then. Bend when you feel it will lead to a long-term relationship and future sales. Like it or not, learning to sell and learning to negotiate is as much art as it is science. If you wish to learn how to build relationships, sell, and negotiate, you may need to spend time with successful sales professionals, read books, and then make some mistakes. Some of the best lessons are learned from our mistakes.

Learn How to Motivate Yourself: The life of the entrepreneur is not always perfect. In fact, some days it can be downright difficult to get motivated. It can be a lot like a crap sandwich you are forced to eat to get to where you want to be. This can be especially true as you are starting out. Often your planned steppingstones feel more like tripping hazards. While no method will work all the time, there are a few ideas which should help to motivate you, if needed. First, always have a list of your personal and business goals with you. Keep the list in a binder, on a smartphone, or on a tablet you can quickly look at and read. When rejections happen and challenges occur, read your goals, and remember what you are working to achieve. Second, keep a picture of the people you are working for (for me, it is always my family) or something you want to buy as the background picture on your smartphone. When the going gets tough and your goals are not enough to inspire you, use the picture to remind you who or what you are really working for. These are the people who are counting on you to become financially free. If you decide to use a picture of something you want to buy, keep in mind it is not the thing you want, but the freedom to buy it debt free. I know it may seem that having a picture of an object you want to buy may seem covetous in nature. If, however, the focus is on your goal and not the thing, then the picture is just a representation of what you want to accomplish. Like most things in life, it ultimately comes down to what your heart is set on. Ironically, you may find when you have worked to reach your goal you may not actually want that item anymore.

Do Not Be a Dummy, Admit You Do Not Know, and Ask for Help: For some reason one of the underdeveloped skills in many entrepreneurs is the ability to admit when they do not know something. Small business owners who smarten up and realize they do not have to know everything end up a lot happier. Nobody but God knows everything, so do not even try. Sure, you need to be a mile wide and a mile deep. You may even want to be 10 miles wide and 10 miles deep.

That is perfectly admirable. What is not admirable is the entrepreneur who tanks their business for a month to file sales taxes because they are too dumb or stubborn to ask for help. Be prudent and use good judgment. Recognize when you do not know and find an expert to help you.

In most metropolitan areas, there are small business networking groups, chambers of commerce, and US Small Business Administration (SBA) offices where you can find someone who can help you. Do not go to your poor Uncle Jack and ask for business advice just because it is free. You usually get your money's worth when you take free advice.

Skills Development is for Everything: Do not limit your development of new talents to what your business does. As you develop new skills and talents, you are likely to find your new skills open up new business and networking opportunities. Do not hesitate to be involved in theater, church service, or to take music lessons. The best entrepreneurs are committed tinkerers. These individuals are not satisfied with succeeding in just one area of their life. When they take up fitness hobbies and other pastimes, they do so with gusto. You will find a lot of the discipline learned building a business will translate to other aspects of your life. You may very well find a new passion that allows you to be more focused when you go back to your business. In my personal life, I have found bicycling, CrossFit, and backpacking does that for me. It gives me a time to clear my mind, stay in shape, and be refreshed mentally.

As a sustainable entrepreneur, you are in control of what you learn and what you do. Remember, you cannot develop personally or in your business if you are spending all your time with those people with no skills or ambition. They will only keep you down. Eagles learn to fly not by roosting with chickens. They learn to fly by observing, and then practicing the skills taught by adult eagles. Who is the eagle you wish to be like? What skills are you developing to become like them so you can fly like they do!

Sometimes the worst critics and naysayers are the people closest to you. Sometimes they are even your family. The reality is sometimes you need to separate yourself from them to make your entrepreneurial dreams come true. I am not implying divorce your spouse and leave your kids. I think families are far too important for that, and we already have enough throwaway things in our society. Your family should not be one of those things. If your family is a naysayer to your ambitions, maybe there is something in your character that would keep you from being a successful entrepreneur. Ask them what it is and if you can, and you can, change it. People change every day and entrepreneurs sometimes change and improve daily or by the minute. Fix the character flaw and then get your family on board with your vision. If your spouse loved you enough to marry you, then they saw potential in you. Prove to them that it was not misplaced. Inspire yourself if you must. Just get off your butt and prove you are made of the right stuff, and you can be a successful, sustainable entrepreneur.

Section 4: Building a Foundation and Action Plan

In the previous sections of this book, we discussed each of the elements of the freedom matrix. Each of the previous chapters included a discussion and reason for each of the eight elements within the matrix. In this section, we will discuss a critical binding element that provides the cohesive glue that makes the freedom matrix work. Additionally, we will discuss the next steps in your journey.

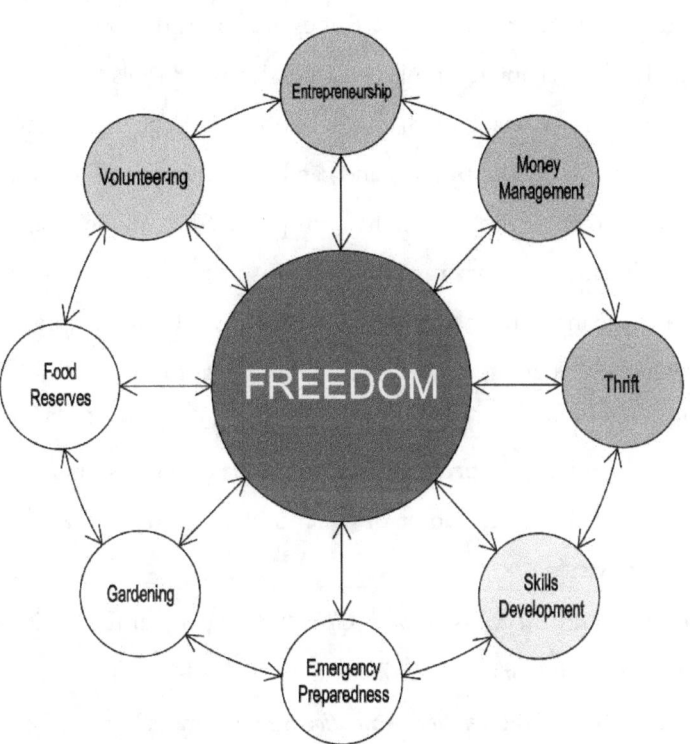

Chapter 9: Pillar to Success: Recognize a Higher Power

In each of the chapters of this book, we described tools for professional and personal growth and development. Each of the tools is important and powerful by itself and can have a massive effect on the small business owner who applies them properly. When all the tools are used in conjunction, the synergy is powerful. It helps those who apply them to mature into a truly sustainable entrepreneur. In this chapter, we are going to talk about the pillar or binding agent to all these tools. This pillar is the foundation upon which you can build at any level of your business and in your personal life. Before we cover this final tool; however, we need to review some of the critical components that make this tool so powerful.

An American Business Health Checkup: Each year the National Center for Education Statistics, a division of the US Department of Education, produces the *Digest of Education Statistics* annual report on education in the United States. The latest report dated August 2023 states, "In 2020–21, postsecondary institutions conferred 5.2 million awards, ranging from certificates below the associate's level to doctor's degrees". Business ranks in the top three programs per enrollment for undergraduate and graduate degrees. In the year 2020-2021 there was a total of 593,700 degrees conferred when combined. Taken over the course of a decade or more, that is a lot of potential business experts in the United States. Yet, with all this professional business education, there is still a massive problem with corporate honesty. Despite this, US corporations generally enjoy favorable public opinion. The question then remains, why do businesses which employ highly trained and educated professionals have such poor public perception when it comes to believability of what they say? The key can be found in two words – honesty and integrity. In the name of inclusivity and never wanting to offend personal religious or non-religious employees and customers, many businesses have moved away from the tried-and-true virtues of honesty and integrity if it is encapsulated within morality.

Believe in Something Bigger: Business schools teach ethics but do so without recognition of God. Educational institutions are so concerned about offending someone they have forgotten a vital piece of the ethical puzzle. Individuals, communities, businesses, and nations fail when a belief in a higher authority is forgotten. The purpose of this book is not to convert you to a particular belief system. However, a belief in something beyond the here-and-now is the pillar of all human self-improvement and growth. If we are accountable to no one than why is honesty so important? To what purpose would we need to have integrity? It is only with our acceptance of inevitable eternal accountability that ethics has any lasting roots.

Use Your Belief in a Higher Power for Needed Strength: As a sustainable entrepreneur, you need something to sustain you. You need to be able to lean on a power that is wiser and more merciful than you are. As your own boss in your own business, you do not have to be bashful about your beliefs. It is not wise to force your beliefs on your customers, but you can always share a little through you actions of honesty and integrity. In truth, your beliefs are personal and how you act and interact with others should always reflect those beliefs. You should not be afraid to use your faith to strengthen you in times of need. After all, our beliefs are the roots of our ethics and make us who we are.

If you feel hesitant about using your faith in your business practices, just stop for a moment and perform a reality check. Despite all the media hype about atheists being offended, remember 81% of Americans believe in God even if they are not actively religious. In short, most people will not be offended if you express your feelings on faith and that you have been blessed to be an entrepreneur. You do not have to apologize if you believe in a higher power. Use it as a daily strength and move forward on a sure foundation.

Gratitude is the Attitude of Altitude: Gratitude for what you have even in times of debt, doubt, and despair is liberating. As a busy business owner (either part-time or full-time), take time every day to express gratitude for what you have been blessed with. Sometimes the challenges can seem unbearable and insurmountable. However, when gratitude is used, instead of despair, amazing things happen. When we are focused on the positive, we are more likely to find solutions and have greater financial success. Daily expression of gratitude helps us to lift our mood and enhance our outlook. It causes us to look at others in a positive light instead of a diminutive shadow. Finally, it helps us to realize that setbacks are not permanent unless we give up. Maintaining gratitude makes it difficult to give up and quit.

Acknowledging a Higher Power Keeps Us Humble: When we accept our nothingness, we keep ourselves humble even if we are successful. There is nothing worse than a human being who believes they are better than everyone else, or that they are fully self-made. In literature and life, the same thing happens to these characters. They are marginalized and eventually we applaud when they exit the scene. The most inspiring human beings are those that despite all they have accomplished are humble, approachable, and real. Relationships built by inspiring individuals and built on trust are real and long lasting. The sustainable entrepreneur who recognizes a higher power will naturally gravitate towards being an inspiration to others.

Things to Consider: Harvard Business Review found entrepreneurs generally feel closer to God than the public at large. Perhaps it is a reflection of recognizing they do not know everything. Many successful entrepreneurs dedicate a time every day for reading from religious texts, to pray, or to meditate. And finally, they typically are more likely to give to charities or religious organizations.

Tithing – Pillar to Success: In the strictest definition *to tithe*, a Judeo-Christian term, is to donate one-tenth of something to a religious organization. However, donations like tithing are not just a Jewish or Christian ideal. In your faith, it may be called Zakāt, Daswandh, giving alms, or offerings, but it is in essence the same thing. It is recognizing a higher power and charitably donating. These kinds of faith-based tithes are given not for recognition but because we believe that some money should be returned to God or in his name to help others. (For the sake of simplicity, we will call all these charitable donations tithing.) So, why on earth should an entrepreneur who is trying to get out of debt pay tithing? The answer is we need to give back for all the blessings we get. Being an entrepreneur is a lot of fun! We are a blessed group of people that make a difference in our customers' lives, our communities, and our family's life. Paying tithing is really one of the simplest ways to acknowledge our gratitude.

Donating 10% of our income to a church, synagogue, mosque, or houses of worship from where we get our spiritual guidance is a small price to pay. The great equity in this is that no matter where we are or how successful we become a set 10% will never be more than 10%. Paying a tithe sets us apart from other businesses. It helps us to recognize we are reliant on a higher power to help us start, build, maintain, and grow our business. Paying tithing enables us to put things in priority. It forces us to be humble and to remember there are many people who are less fortunate than we are. It enables God to trust us with more so we can do more positive in the world. Finally, it gives us a way to enable the laws of attraction.

The laws of attraction are called many different things. Basically, it means that we reap what we sow. This concept is found in nearly every religious doctrine and self-help program. It is doing good to God and others results in blessings and peace in our own life. When we are willing to loosen our grip on possessions and give to God, we are also more willing to take the needed risks to be a successful sustainable entrepreneur. Risk becomes less terrifying when we feel the hand of divine providence guiding us. When we know and understand God knows the answers to everything, we know we can rely on Him to help us harness our fears. We can then lean on Him for what we need to know. With this understanding, we begin to see tithing is not about money, but about the application and acceptance of our individual faith and our need for spiritual guidance.

Chapter 10: The First Step

The Chinese philosopher and poet Lao-Tzu said, "The journey of a thousand miles begins with one step." In this book, we have talked about the steppingstones or tools available to you on your journey to becoming a sustainable entrepreneur. It was designed to help you take your first steps towards achieving your dream of financial freedom through small business ownership and lifestyle adjustments. As with any journey, this one will begin when you take the first step. Make your plan and be willing to change your plan as you move forward. Set your goals and do not assume you will be able to perfectly predict the future. Success often comes in different disguises. They key is to never adjust your values and personal mission statement.

You are the captain of the ship of your life. You have been created for great things and with infinite potential. As you achieve your goals, remember to continue to stretch yourself further. If your desire is to become debt free - go for it. You deserve it and have the right to achieve it through your ambition and hard work. Remember you have an obligation to give to others and acknowledge the blessings freedom affords you. Do not forget to reach back and mentor someone else. Let them join you in your journey as a sustainable entrepreneur.

Not Ready, Yet: Begin now to take the steps to make your business idea a reality. If you are not ready to start your business yet, then begin to set the other elements of the freedom matrix into motion. In time, you will find having a garden and food reserves can help when budgets are tight. Developing your skills and volunteering can help you prepare and refine your abilities so you can develop your business ideas. There are always benefits to good money management and thrift. These are patterns for living that can help you to save money now so your business idea can be funded if funding is needed. In short, you do not have to be ready today to begin your journey toward becoming a sustainable entrepreneur. You can begin to set in motion all the elements of the freedom matrix so you can live the life you want to live, be the boss you want to work for, and build the dream business you want to build.

Epilogue

This book is the result of a lot of years of self-discovery and lessons learned. As anyone who has ever taken on a task of this kind knows, there are always so many considerations. The first consideration is how can a guy still on this journey for himself author a book like this? Great question! It is one that stopped me from completing this book for nearly a decade. I kept telling myself I could not present myself as an expert unless I had perfected my own execution. A funny thought hit me one day, and I knew it was time to complete this book. I have come to realize there are really very few real experts. I often read or hear a news story and my response is the same, 'this person is putting themselves out there as an expert and they are full of nonsense.' These "experts" are consulted with repeatedly to know what their analysis is even when reality and facts do not line up with what they present. So, let me complete this thought with a couple of few key points 1) I am not an expert and I do not claim to be; 2) the opinions expressed here are my own and reflect my own beliefs and experience; and 3) this is not expected to be an academic study on entrepreneurship success.

Ultimately, this book is the result of me taking into account there are a lot of lessons learned I should share now even if the ideas are not perfected. Just as I do with my business ideas, I need to be less timid about sharing them and be more open about my own shortcomings in the process. Perhaps reading this book and these final thoughts will inspire you to do what you need to do and what perhaps you have been putting off while you waited for the right time.

Brian Allen

About the Author

Brian Allen has more than 30 years of leadership experience in international operations and project management. His broad experience includes leadership and sales experience in information technology, ecommerce, telecommunications, international sales and operations management, and international project management. Brian has a Doctor of Business Administration in Technology Entrepreneurship degree, an MBA, and Master of Project Management. He is dedicated full-time educator of current and future business and healthcare leaders. Brian and his wife are proud US Air Force veterans. They are the proud parents of six children and four grandchildren.